Rhetorical Criticism
A Study in Method

EDWIN BLACK

The University of Wisconsin Press

Published 1978

The University of Wisconsin Press
114 North Murray Street
Madison, Wisconsin 53715

The University of Wisconsin Press, Ltd.
1 Gower Street
London WC1E 6HA, England

Wisconsin printings 1978, 1979

Originally published in 1965
by The Macmillan Company

Printed in the United States of America
ISBN 0-299-07550-8 cloth, 0-299-07554-0 paper
LC 77-91050

To Herbert A. Wichelns

CONTENTS

Author's Foreword   ix

Preface   xvii

Chapter   I   *The Meaning of Criticism*   1

Chapter   II   *The Practice of Rhetorical Criticism*   10

Chapter III   *Rhetoric and General Criticism*   36

Chapter IV   *Aristotle and Rhetorical Criticism*   91

Chapter   V   *An Alternative Frame of Reference*   132

Chapter VI   *The Genre of Argumentation*   148

vii

AUTHOR'S FOREWORD

Rhetorical Criticism, A Study in Method was initially published in 1965 by the Macmillan Company and it was extensively reviewed in the months following its appearance. Reviewers were immoderately divided in their assessments of the book, but most of them agreed in predicting that it would provoke controversy among its readers. The prophecy proved correct.

After the depletion of the first printing the publisher chose to let the book expire, but it continued an elusive, marginal existence in photocopies, mimeographed excerpts, and footnoted allusions—a subject of fitful but chronic dispute. Being unobtainable, the book did not live, but it would not quite die either. It became after a while a spectral rumor of a book haunting the shadows of rhetorical criticism, an eristic ghost equivocal only in its own mortality. The very persistence of that half life has prompted the University of Wisconsin Press to undertake this new printing, in the hope that it is a revival the Press is sponsoring and not the exhumation of a deceptively twitching corpse.

Even now, dead or alive, this book is certain to affect different readers in different ways, but it cannot recapitulate its original impact because the methods by which rhetorical criticism is practiced have changed since 1965. There is less uniformity in the techniques of rhetorical criticism and in the sorts of subjects deemed appropriate to it, less agreement on its proper role or its ideal condition, more contention, more experiment, more confusion, more vitality. For good or ill, this book has been involved in some of those changes and so it represents now what it could not have represented in its first printing: an episode in the modern history of its own subject. Out of that consideration the book is reissued without alteration of its original text except for the correction of typographical errors—all minor—and the addition of this introductory note.

Behind the composition of *Rhetorical Criticism, A Study in Method* was an idea that was too dimly understood by its author to possess the book as firmly as it would if the book were to be written now. That idea is that critical method is too personally expressive to be systematized.

Our intellectual world contains various methods, variously distinguishable. Methods may be discriminated by their precision, their productiveness, their complexity, their comprehensiveness, and so forth. The distinction among methods that is of concern here is based on the degree of their objectivity—on the extent to which they require or foreclose personal choices.

There are some methods that are so completely independent of personality, they can be regarded as wholly objective. One example would be the method of determining circumference from diameter. It is true, of course, that an ebullient geometrist might contrive to express some elements of his personality in the calculation, but such an expression would be superfluous to the method. No personal choices could enhance or detract from the method of determining a circumference as that method has come to be understood.

There are some methods whose practitioners aspire to the condition of objectivity, but that are subject to contingencies and so retain a component of personality. Surgery is an example. Although a given surgical procedure—an appendectomy or a tonsillectomy—may involve routine and well understood techniques, an incalculable number of unforeseeable contingencies could require the spontaneously creative intervention of the surgeon.

And finally, there are methods that require personal choices at every step, methods that are pervaded by contingencies. Composing a sonata is an example. The predetermined and impersonal component of musical composition may consist of little more than the generic form with which the final product comports. One may be able to say subsequent to an act of composition, "This is a sonata that has been composed," but one may be unable to describe any of the procedures that figured in the composition. Methods, then, admit of varying degrees of personality. And criticism, on the whole, is near the indeterminate, contingent, personal end of the methodological scale. In consequence of this placement, it is neither possible nor desirable for criticism to be fixed into a system, for critical techniques to be objectified, for critics to be interchangeable for purposes of replication, or for rhetorical criticism to serve as the handmaiden of quasi-scientific theory.

Certainly, criticism is not uniform in its character. Some criticism strives for impersonality and may even achieve an illusion of objectivity. Other criticism is presented in a strongly personal voice and leaves its readers with a distinct impression of the critic's perceiving mind. But taking criticism all together, it has historically displayed two characteristics that associate it with an interpretive, morally colored perspective on inquiry. These characteristics are first, that a specific person—the critic—is the sole instrument of observation; and second, that the style of critical writing is intrinsic to criticism. These two characteristics are interrelated, but each may be considered separately.

To note that in critical inquiry the critic is the sole instrument of observation is to note a defining characteristic. Other, more nearly objective methods can often be served by instruments of measurement or of optical or auditory enhancement that augment, confirm, or even sometimes replace purely human perception. In criticism, however, although all knowledge gained by whatever means has to be held potentially useful, there are no instruments that mediate the engagement between the critic and his subject. That engagement is and has historically been a direct one, and to the extent it became indirect, it would cease being criticism.

A critical instrument in the present context does not refer only to the gauges, dials, and reproductions of mechanical apparatus. The term also, more germanely, refers to methodological systems or programs—to neo-Aristotelian criticism or Burkean criticism or phenomenological criticism or structuralist criticism—to the formation of critical method into rules or taxonomy. It refers to any a priori procedure.

Because only the critic is the instrument of criticism, the critic's relationship to other instruments will profoundly affect the value of critical inquiry. And in criticism, every instrument has to be assimilated to the critic, to have become an integral part of the critic's mode of perception. A critic who is influenced by, for example, the Burkean pentad and who, in consequence of that influence, comes to see some things in a characteristically dramatistic way—that critic is still able to function in his own person as the critical instrument, and so the possibility of significant disclosure remains open to him. But the would-be critic who has not internalized the pentad, who undertakes to "use" it as a mathematician would use a formula—such a critic is certain (yes, *certain!*) to produce work that is sterile. An act of criticism conducted on mechanistic assumptions will, not surprisingly, yield mechanistic criticism.

The relationship between the inquirer and his method is not a consequential matter in all realms of study. We do not expect a chemist to have assimilated a laboratory procedure. Indeed, although we would respect the chemist for ably executing the procedure, we would expect him to sustain a degree of detachment from it. In fact, we are ordinarily indifferent to the chemist's attitude towards his techniques, for the techniques have become objectified instruments and they are supposed to function so as to prevent the chemist's personal qualities from affecting the experiment. The case of criticism is otherwise.

We manifest in various ways our implicit view of criticism as a personal instrument. For example, we do not value criticism that apprehends an object the way anyone else could equally well apprehend it or in a way that is predictable or conventional. In criticism, as in art, we value originality and the marks of skills so integrally mastered that they are exercised with the grace of full possession. We value criticism that gives us *singular* access to its subject.

To say that criticism is a personal instrument is not to say that it is a private one. The critic does address a public and he thereby incurs public responsibilities. The critic's public should, in principle, be able to verify for itself that the critical object can be apprehended as the critic proposes without offending reason, and that the critic's way of apprehending the object yields moral understanding of it. Those are not standards that can be satisfied by self-indulgent, impressionistic, confessional, or shallow criticism. But neither are they standards that presuppose a radical disparity between personal experience and public significance.

(When I wrote *Rhetorical Criticism, A Study in Method,* I was much too sure of the distinction between statements about the world and statements about oneself. I attributed public significance to the former, but not to the latter. I was wrong. I now understand better that even reflexive statements make claims on their auditors and that our private experience cannot be divorced from our social history. Therefore, my present conception of criticism would put more emphasis than this book did on the personal requisites for the task of criticism and on the scruples that refine the critic's perceptions.)

It is the public responsibility of the critic that makes style intrinsic to criticism. The function of criticism in shaping the ways in which an object will be apprehended brings the style of critical writing to transcend mere embellishment, and to acquire probative force.

Style is a manifestation of personality. Where we find in any human activity symptoms of personal choices and decisions concerning the method of that activity, we regard those symptoms as style. And in any method, the importance of style will be exactly correlated with the subjectivity of the method.

Those disciplines that seek objectivity as an ideal characteristically develop modes of discourse from which style has been purged. In experimental psychology, for example, there is a widely accepted formula for reporting experiments. The formula admits of little variation; it inhibits any sort of personal expression except in a subsection usually called "discussion," and even there the expression of personality is supposed to be very circumspect. The language of such reports effaces personality through the extensive use of passive sentences and neologisms constituting a technical vocabulary.

Such writing has sometimes been attacked for its ugliness, but its ugliness is functional. The writing is supposed to be impersonal, it is supposed to distance the reader rather than enchant him, it is supposed to be purged of attitude and sentiment. It is designed to be a datum rather than the projection of a human voice, and so to be capable of integration into the corpus of ordered data that constitutes the discipline itself.

The ideal of objectivity beckons some methods of inquiry to seek a language of pure denotation and pure relationship, free of the remotest hint of personality. Mathematics represents the achievement of such a quest for some disciplines. Others, that still must retain a language of common speech, try to reshape it to the mathematical ideal: impersonal, value-free, unambiguous, transparent. So draconic a language is vulnerable to the judgment of being aesthetically offensive.

By contrast, critiques are a kind of discourse that acts as an extension of a writer—an autonomous surrogate for a human voice. A critique represents a particular mind at work on an object: apprehending it, examining it, coming to understand it, placing it into history. A function of such writing is to bring its reader to corroborate an interpretive process—not necessarily the same one that the critic has experienced but in any case one that will finally bring the reader to the interpretation that the critique proposes. If the interpretation is at all nuanced, if it is shaded and complex (which is to say, *interesting*), then its presentation will depend on subtleties of style that are highly individuated. Patently, such criticism requires critics who have mastered its techniques.

Competence in surgery requires skill in the use of the scalpel. Competence in carpentry requires skill in the use of the hammer. Competence in violin-playing requires skill in the use of the bow. And competence in criticism requires skill in the use of its indispensable tool, the language.

These reflections on the subjectivity of criticism are recorded here as a corrective to this book's excessive deference, especially in its first chapter, to an ideal of objectivity. Are there other emendations I would propose for this book? No, not really: not because I think the book incorrigible, but rather because there is a sense in which I am not any longer the one who wrote this book. I knew its author well, but I sometimes have trouble remembering him.

This book is, after all, not only about rhetorical criticism, it is also a series of critical acts. And so whatever is the case with criticism is also the case with this book. It is pervaded by an authorial persona whose choices mark every page. It is a persona whose identity now is wholly contained by the book. As Plato observed of writing, this persona cannot answer interrogators, but neither can anyone quite answer for him. Books have to stand on their own.

This book was originally dedicated to Herbert Wichelns. It now, alas, must be dedicated to his memory. My sense of indebtedness to him has abided through these years, undiminished.

E. B.

Madison, Wisconsin
September 1977

PREFACE

Of all the responses a book can evoke, none is so obituary as silence. A treatise is, after all, nothing if not a statement, and even the humblest statement implicitly courts its counterstatement. Yet, no books seem to inspire a deathlike hush so dependably as those on the subject of rhetoric. Aristole's *Rhetoric,* for the supreme example, instead of initiating the vigorous discussion and exploration of the subject that are the symptoms of a viable tradition, was followed—with pitifully few exceptions—by two millennia of feeble echoes and the babbling murmur of second-rate minds, finally moving Welldon in the nineteenth century to remark the *Rhetoric* as "a solitary instance of a book which not only begins a science but completes it." It is not hard to imagine Welldon writing his comment in a sardonic mood.

More recently Thonssen and Daird's admirable book, *Speech Criticism,* was published, and gave substance to the suspicion that the field of rhetoric had, in truth, not only a subject matter of its own, but a scholarly method as well. The practice of rhetorical criticism is by no means still where Thonssen and Baird found it in 1948, but the theoretical statements that have appeared in the intervening years have been too few, and many of those few too concise, with the result that there is an almost universal discontent in the profession—perhaps its surest sign of life.

This volume is an attempt to stimulate and expand the dialogue on rhetorical criticism. It has been written in the belief that variety is wanting in the methods of rhetoric, that the options available to the critic need to be multiplied, and above all, that the prevailing mode of rhetorical criticism is profoundly mistaken. This book has its genesis, then, in dissatisfaction—not a singular emotion, if one may judge from the growing literature of professional protest and vocational self-analysis in the speech journals. The character of that genesis has left its marks on this book, giving it an assertively trumpeted point of view. That assertiveness is the product of conscious choice, for the methods of rhetorical criticism ought to be argued about, and none would know better than students of rhetoric the values of controversy.

The orientation of this book is methodological rather than historical, and it is aimed at the advanced student rather than the beginner. Its examples of criticism have been drawn extensively from essays in the three volumes of *A History and Criticism of American Public Address,* which some readers may want to employ for supplemental purposes.

I owe great debts to many people for the making of this book. Carroll C. Arnold gave me an insightful reading of an earlier version of the manuscript and offered suggestions that have been of great value. My chairman at the University of Pittsburgh, Jack Matthews, has, in his usual generous way, made available to me every resource he could command to free my time, facilitate my writing, and gladden my spirits. Also at the University of Pittsburgh, my students in the seminar in Rhetorical Criticism have patiently suffered rehearsals of most of the ideas explored here, and have given me the stimulus of their candor. I am grateful, too, to Mrs. Elizabeth Ann Magasano, who has done a beautiful job of typing the manuscript.

The preeminent debt is that I owe my teacher, to whom this book is dedicated. If there is any positive merit here, it can be laid to his influence.

There remain in this volume ideas that represent the author's stubborn insistence. They are here contrary to the friendliest of advice. Thus it is that I alone am responsible for the blunders.

E. B.

University of Pittsburgh
1965

Rhetorical Criticism

A Study in Method

CHAPTER I

The Meaning
of Criticism

THE SCIENTIST is one of the cultural heroes of our age. He is consulted by senators, courted by corporations, and exalted by the popular mind. It is no wonder that we respect the office of scientist, for one mystery after another has yielded to the formidable machinery of scientific method. And with the mysteries, so also numberless human afflictions are closer to our control: hunger and squalor, pain and neurotic anguish, enervating toil and terrifying superstition, perhaps, as Bergson once dared hope, even death itself. Having, as it sometimes seems, the key to the universe in its very techniques of investigation, science is on a progress of discovery that has no conceivable limit, unless it is the mushroom cloud on the horizon. The triumphs of science seem inexorable as the tide.

This quest is both the glory and terror of the race, and one of its effects has been to make scientific methodology a model for thought, so that Pater's famous phrase can, with some truth, be paraphrased: all intellection aspires to the condition of physics. Scholars in all branches of learning are called upon for increasing precision of thought, clarity of expression, and refinement of methodology. These demands are not invariably met, but their persistence is invariably felt, and by the critic no less than by others.

There are, no doubt, certain disadvantages to science's having become, at least to the public at large, the model for intellectual activity, but on the whole the influence of scientific method on criticism has probably been wholesome. If nothing else, this influence has tended to make modern critics especially conscious of their methods. It has encouraged critics to become systematic, to objectify their modes of inquiry, and to restrict themselves to demonstrable, or at least arguable, generalizations.

Thus, the modern critic has assumed the burden not only of understanding and evaluating the products of human effort, but also of defining and delimiting the nature of his own criticism. He performs his tasks aware of the recalcitrant mystery of the work he seeks to render and, what is more remarkable, aware of competing, sometimes mutually exclusive approaches to the work's rendering. The labor of the contemporary critic serves both to disclose the enigmas of an artistic product and to sanction, implicity or overtly, its own methods of disclosure.

Such professional self-consciousness has not always been characteristic of criticism. The critics of classical antiquity, whether composing rhetorics, poetics, or histories of art, seemed uninterested in reflecting on their own activities. To articulate the principles of Sophoclean tragedy or Roman forensic oratory was, for Aristotle and Cicero, the end and justification of their respective critical works. They assumed the mission of elevating intuitive acts of creation to the status of viable method. Their aim was to formulate technical principles that artists could use: to make creativity systematic. They wrote primarily, not for the critic himself, or for the auditor, but for the artist. One searches the ancient critics in vain for an explanation of critical procedure. That sort of work was left for their more recent successors. Aristotle could define the scope and technique of the deliberative orator, but he did not write on the scope and technique of the critic of deliberative oratory. Generally, the critics of antiquity did not theorize about criticism. The focus of their scrutiny was on the work of the artist, not on one another. That criticism itself could become a systematic methodology seems not to have occurred to our early critical precursors.

In this ingenuousness of ancient criticism we can glimpse the ethos of a simpler world. The scholarship of antiquity was not divided into the arbitrary jigsaw puzzle of departments or disciplines, which freed the ancient critic of the burden of self-justification. His work was redeemed by the quality of its execution; its distinctiveness was of no consequence.

Later critics, having to deal with more diverse variations in artistic production and with a vastly increased quantity of art objects, have found it necessary to adopt both more modest and more ambitious aspirations than their predecessors. The modesty has been in their efforts at carving scholarship into self-sufficient and independent units, making for greater specialization by critics, and inducing each critic to take a smaller fragment of the world as his field. The ambition lay in the attempt to create an articulate methodology where before there had been only the naïve and direct thrust for enlightenment in a study.

The sense of history itself has encouraged our modern auto-criticism. The immense proliferation of artifacts for century after century in a civilization acutely concerned with keeping records of its own past, and endowed with the technical means of accumulating and preserving these records, presents the contemporary critic with an enormous quantity of material to be discriminated and interpreted. The critic, in his turn, must specialize or be engulfed.

We are, then, in an age of critical self-consciousness and specialization. Critics discriminate special types and areas of criticism which they essay to define, circumscribe, justify, and enrich. Just one such area or type is rhetorical criticism, the subject of this book, and our present task is to illuminate rhetorical criticism. Yet, before we can come to understand the special case of criticism as applied in rhetoric, we first must understand the general enterprise that criticism is.

Criticism is that which critics do. This is one way of answering the question, What is criticism? It is, on its surface, a sportive, perhaps even a suspiciously evasive answer; yet, functional definitions are occasionally useful to inquiry, and however empty this answer may at first appear, it does commit us to a certain approach. It compels us to focus on the critic.

One does not see on his television screen the image of the critic, suitably costumed in the critic's version of a white smock (a judicial gown, perhaps?), exploited to sell toothpaste. The scientific image is more fashionable. Yet, the critic is not so different from the scientist as one might suppose. Both have in common two vitally important activities, which are to see a thing clearly and to record what they have seen precisely. Beyond these activities, which might serve as a greatly simplified characterization of the means of science, we need add only one other item to complete the snapshot of the critic: he also seeks to judge the thing justly.

The scientist is not interested in judging; not in his capacity as scientist. He will have the tastes of other men, of course. He will be subject to boredom, to fascination, to delight, to all the affections and repulsions accessible to humanity at large, but not in the laboratory. The scientist, qua scientist, does not love, hate, or evaluate. He investigates, he measures, he verifies. His impulse is exploratory. He seeks a method of investigation which will ignore the vagaries of his own temperament and be unaffected by his values. His neutrality is his pride.

The critic shares many of these characteristics. At his best, he too tries to become, for a time, a pure perceiver, an undistorting slate on which an object or an event external to him can leave a faithful impression of itself, omitting nothing. But this percipient purity is only a phase in the critical process, not its totality. Beyond perception is appraisal; beyond seeing a thing is attaching a value to it. These two acts—perception and evaluation—distinguishable as they are in theory, are generally experienced as inseparable phases of the same process. That process is criticism.

It is not in the act of evaluation alone that the critic differs from the scientist. There are at least two other distinctions between them. One of these distinctions is implied by observing that criticism is a humanistic activity. That is to say, criticism is concerned with humanity. The scientist typically studies natural phenomena. He is interested in all events in nature. Sometimes he is able to produce or duplicate these events in his laboratory, and thus more easily come to understand them, and frequently there emerges as a consequence of scientific activity the subjugation of natural phenomena to human control and exploitation. But the subject of scientific investigation is not ordinarily the contrived event or the controlled phenomenon itself. It is nature spontaneous.

The critic, on the other hand, studies the products of man. Whether in painting or city planning, poetry or pottery, music or mosaics, the subject of criticism is always some harvest of the human imagination. There are no critics of stars, however beautiful; there are only astronomers. The subject of criticism consists exclusively in human activities and their results.

The final trait of the critic distinguishing him from the scientist is the critic's interest in making his criticism a force in society. Again, we must make our distinction between the ideals, the aspirations of the two professions. Certainly no one living in the Atomic Age can doubt the social impact of scientific investigation, nor should one neglect the human and sometimes humane motives that drive the scientist. Yet, the scientist, as a scientist, does not address himself to any public except the community of his professional peers. The popular dissemination of his findings is in the nature of a postscript; it is the afterthought of exploration, but not a part of its essence.

The critic's circumstance is otherwise. He occupies the office of mediator, receiving from one source and conveying to another. The critic proceeds in part by translating the object of his criticism into the terms of his audience and in part by educating his audience to the terms of the object. This dual task is not an ancillary function of criticism; it is an essential part of criticism.

However esoterically a critic may write—and some critics write very badly—he is always an interpreter, and he means to affect the way in which his own auditor will apprehend the object of his criticism. An essay on *Hamlet* that makes no difference whatever to anybody's understanding or appreciation of *Hamlet*, and affects nobody's response to *Hamlet*, would be a failure as criticism. The nullity of such an essay's effects would have had to be caused by its incomprehensibility, or its vacuity, or its wrongness, and any of those attributes is fatal to criticism. This certainly does not mean that the merit of a critique can be established by its popularity, or that the setters of fashion are necessarily the best critics. It does mean, though, that the critic is an educator, and insofar as he fails to educate, he fails his essential office. However restricted an audience the critic chooses to address, however high the standards of admission to his school, he means to teach, and in this respect his task is distinguishable from the ideal of science, which is only to discover.[1]

This comparison and contrast between criticism and science has been purely conceptual. It has assumed the ideal of each enterprise. In fact, the scientist is as subject to human frailty as the rest of us, and rarely so detached and disinterested as the image his profession projects. Similarly, much criticism is aborted, and either bungles or ignores some of its essential work. We will, in the pages to follow, confront the actual practice of criticism. It is enough now to prepare for that confrontation by gaining a perspective. The means of gaining that perspective— the comparison of criticism with science—has been more than merely a capricious simile. If, with the exceptions noted, criti-

---

[1] Cf. Anthony Hillbruner, "Criticism as Persuasion," *The Southern Speech Journal*, XXVIII (Summer 1963), pp. 260–267.

cism is comparable to science, then certain vital implications follow for our general characterization of criticism. The scientist is one who is associated with scientific method. He is, in sum, committed to adhere to certain strict procedures of logic, and to certain well-defined intellectual values. A man who dogmatized, who insisted stubbornly on the truth of his own claims irrespective of contrary evidence, would be violating a scientific value. He would, in his dogmatism, be unscientific. A man who made assertions of fact and refused to justify those assertions with empirical evidence would be unscientific. A man who, in the guise of reporting an event, reported his perception of the event without troubling to guarantee the accuracy of his perception would be unscientific. A man who composed pseudo-objective autobiography—who reported events that occurred inside his skin as if they had occurred outside his skin—would be unscientific. All of these are violations of the morality that governs scientific activity and that, in the end, may constitute the clearest definition of scientific method. The pages to follow will assume the relevance of the same morality in criticism.

There are statements sometimes taken for criticism that, because they violate one or another of the scruples governing criticism, will not be interpreted here as critical statements. The person who hears a speech and says, "I like it," is not making a critical statement. He is reporting the state of his glands; he is speaking autobiographically. If we happen to like the person or if we are curious about the state of his glands, we may be interested in his report. Certainly his psychoanalyst would be interested in it. But neither the analyst nor we should confuse the statement with criticism. It is not criticism because, although it may be stimulated by an object, it is not *about* an object; it is a statement about the speaker's own feelings, and nothing more. There are innumerable variations of this kind of statement, some of them less honestly blunt, some of them masquerading as objective, but none of them is, strictly speaking, criticism.

A critical statement is, in some sense, verifiable. A critical statement, even a critical judgment, is one for which reasons can be given, reasons that may gain the agreement of rational people to the statement. Now a psychological report is not directly verifiable. If a man says that he likes or dislikes something, it is logically similar to his saying that he has a pain in his toe. We cannot see his pain, and we must rely entirely on circumstantial evidence for believing in his pain. Usually, we simply take his word for it. If, after reporting a pain in his toe, we see him dancing strenuously and with enjoyment, we can doubt the reality of his pain. Similarly, if he reports a dislike of something but still contrives to be near that thing, to savor it and display symptoms of being attracted by it, we can doubt that he really dislikes. In both cases, we look for behavior that is compatible with the report, but we cannot see directly whatever is reported. We cannot see it because it is behind the skin of the reporter. The report illuminates the reporter's own sensations, but it does not provide us with information about the object or event that may have provoked those sensations. Knowing this, and knowing also that a person is usually the best judge of his own internal states, we generally accept such reports on faith. We behave unscientifically. There are times when the critic, like the physicist, commits acts of faith: the physicist has faith in the uniformity of nature, the critic in the value of humanity. But neither the physicist nor the critic should expect their inferences or their findings to be accepted on faith. Both carry the burden of proving their claims, and that proof must be of a sort that is accessible to others as proof.

Part of our efforts in considering rhetorical criticism must be to clarify what kinds and standards of proof are appropriate to it. Clearly, we cannot expect to be able to apply intact the standards of science to the enterprise of criticism. The objects of investigation in the two areas are too radically different. Indeed, every distinction we have noted between science and criticism is attributable to the fact that criticism is a humanistic activity—that is, it studies the works of human beings. And this fact implies that the proofs and demonstrations of criticism will have about them a provisionality, even at times a degree of imprecision, that the scientist would not purport to allow. We find considerably less uniformity in the works of men than in the phenomena of nature. Consequently, we have not obtained in criticism the exactness of chemistry or physics, nor can we express even our most confident conclusions in a language that will approach mathematics in its elegance and purity. Even so, we seek in criticism to be as exact as our subject will permit, and the highest attainments of science can remain for the critic, if not models to be copied, then at least achievements to be emulated.

The fact that criticism is a humanistic activity implies more than that it will be less exact than some of the sciences. The fact also implies—or, perhaps more accurately, is implied by— the end, the goal of criticism: the understanding of man himself. The scientist seeks to understand objects and events in nature. If he has any motive beyond the understanding itself, that motive is the hope that nature may be predicted and controlled, to the end that men's power may be extended. By contrast, criticism, like other humanistic studies, seeks to understand men by studying men's acts and creations. If the critic has a motive beyond understanding—and he usually does—that motive is to enhance the quality of human life. This objective may seem to be a sentimental plea for criticism; in fact, it is not. Critics have been known to have cruel and perverse visions of the good life, and men have been known to slaughter one another in their disagreements over the character of human perfection. A noble motive is no guarantee of virtue. We note the humanistic objective of criticism not out of piety, but only that we may record the inextricable involvement of criticism with moral values, a subject that will be explored in a subsequent chapter. What we can now crystalize is a tentative definition of criticism, by way of summary. Criticism is a discipline that, through the investigation and appraisal of the activities and products of men, seeks as its end the understanding of man himself.

How the special application of this discipline has been made in the area of rhetoric, and how it might be made are the subjects to which we next must turn.

CHAPTER II

The Practice
of Rhetorical Criticism

WHAT IS rhetorical criticism? What constitutes its distinctiveness? How, if at all, does it differ from any other sort of criticism? To answer these questions we must examine the general practice of rhetorical criticism.

To begin with the obvious, rhetorical criticism is the criticism of rhetorical discourses. This is not the profoundest of definitions, but it is not without its overtones, and we may profit by lingering on the term "rhetorical discourse." Because rhetorical critics frequently belong to academic departments of speech, rhetorical discourses are sometimes taken to be orations. Not all critics concur in this view.

> From the beginning of publication in writing . . . essentially rhetorical performances, whether already spoken or to be spoken, have been committed to paper and circulated

to be read rather than heard—from Isocrates' *Panathenaicus*
or Christ's *Sermon on the Mount* to Eisenhower's message
on the state of the nation. Furthermore, for centuries now,
especially since the invention and cheapening of the art of
printing, the agitator, the teacher, the preacher, the wielder
of public opinion has used the press quite independently
of the platform. Hence, obviously, rhetoric must be understood to be the rationale of informative and suasory discourse both spoken and written . . .[1]

There is in this argument a needful destruction of the too
tidy distinction between spoken and written discourse. Patently,
the pamphlet of the Watch Tower Society is more closely related to the sermon than to the lyric poem, though it has a
mechanical medium of expression in common with the latter.
Patently, the *Iliad* is more closely related to the novel than to
the ceremonial oration, despite its existence in an oral tradition
for some years before its having been written at last. To equate
rhetorical discourse with spoken discourse produces too many
paradoxes. Whatever else the nature of rhetorical discourse, it
is assuredly not to be confined exclusively to the spoken word.
It is a kind of discourse, simply. The means by which the discourse is disseminated have no bearing on the definition.

Whether we can take rhetorical discourse to be that discourse
which is informative and suasory is open to question. Informative discourse is not usually associated with rhetoric, either historically or at present. It is true that a high proportion of the
current textbooks on public speaking contain treatments of exposition, but the subject is so uniformly absent in the rhetorical
theories of the past and the rhetorical criticism of the present
that its presence in textbooks can be attributed to expedient or
commercial considerations.

In the tradition that can be traced from Plato and Aristotle
through Campbell in the eighteenth century and Whately in the
nineteenth to Kenneth Burke in our own time, only two major

---

[1] Donald C. Bryant, "Rhetoric: Its Functions and Its Scope," *Quarterly
Journal of Speech*, XXXIX (December 1953), p. 407.

writers on rhetoric have involved informative as well as persuasive discourse in their definitions of rhetoric: Quintilian and
Campbell.

Quintilian, in his review of the definitions of rhetoric that his
Greek and Roman predecessors had expounded, found persuasion or persuasive speaking to be the explicit or implied scope
of every one.[2] Though Quintilian's own definition of rhetoric—
"the science of speaking well"[3]—does not confine rhetoric to
persuasive discourse alone, it is only persuasive discourse that
Quintilian has in mind throughout his treatise. Nowhere does
he suggest that "neutral" exposition is a distinctive genre of discourse to be included within the province of rhetoric. His most
systematic treatment of expository speaking makes that type of
address a phase in the development of forensic appeals, always
with a persuasive end in view.[4]

George Campbell opens his treatise by defining eloquence as
"that art or talent by which discourse is adapted to its end,"[5] a
definition which certainly leaves room for expository discourse
to be a part of rhetoric. He goes on to observe: "All the ends of
speaking are reducible to four; every speech intended to enlighten
the understanding, to please the imagination, to move the passions, or to influence the will."[6] But Campbell soon makes it
clear that he does not view these "ends of speaking" as co-
ordinates, which would make expository discourse, designed to
"enlighten the understanding," a part of rhetoric. Rather, Campbell has a hierarchical view of these ends.

> In general it may be asserted, that each preceding species
> in the order above exhibited, is preparatory to the subse-
> quent; that each subsequent species is founded on the

---

[2] Quintilian, *Institutio Oratoria*, H. E. Butler, trans. (London, 1953), bk. ii,
ch. 15.

[3] *Ibid.*, bk. i, p. 319.

[4] *Ibid.*, bk. iv, ch. 2.

[5] George Campbell, *The Philosophy of Rhetoric* (Oxford, England, 1838),
p. 1.

[6] *Ibid.*

preceding; and that thus they ascend in a regular progression. Knowledge, the object of the intellect, furnisheth materials for the fancy; the fancy culls, compounds, and by herminic art, disposes these materials so as to affect the passions; the passions are the natural spurs to volition or action, and so need only to be right directed.[7]

The enlightening of the understanding is, then, a legitimate end of rhetorical discourse to Campbell, but it is an end that interests him only insofar as it obtains a persuasive effect. Campbell's interest is betrayed when he comes to consider the faculties of understanding, imagination, memory, and passion. A scant paragraph is devoted to "understanding," [8] while the other faculties receive considerably fuller treatment.[9] Further, even this paragraph treats of exposition as a preliminary to persuasion.

. . . the first thing to be studied by the speaker is, that his *arguments* be understood. If they be unintelligible, the cause must be either in the sense or in the expression. It lies in the sense, if the *mediums of proof* be such as the hearers are unacquainted with; that is, if the ideas introduced be either without the sphere of their knowledge, or too abstract for their apprehension and habits of thinking. It lies in the sense, likewise, if the train of reasoning (though no unusual ideas should be introduced) be longer, or more complex, or more intricate, than they are accustomed to. But as the *fitness of the arguments* in these respects, depends on the capacity, education, and attainments of the hearers, which in different orders of men are different, this properly belongs to the consideration which the speaker ought to have of his audience, not as men in general, but as such men in particular. The obscurity which ariseth from the expression will come in course to be considered in the sequel.[10]

---

[7] *Ibid.*, p. 2.
[8] *Ibid.*, p. 75.
[9] *Ibid.*, pp. 75–84.
[10] *Ibid.*, p. 75. Italics mine.

The sequel Campbell promises is the sixth chapter of *The Philosophy of Rhetoric*, "Of Perspicuity." It is a chapter full of cogent insights into the causes of obscurity and sound advice on the attainment of clarity in style, but it is not a chapter focussed on expository discourse. Most of the examples Campbell quotes in the chapter are statements with persuasive intent. He makes it clear that he does not associate perspicuity with expository discourse, but regards it as a necessary characteristic of style in any genre, ". . . whatever be the ultimate intention of the orator, to inform, to convince, to please, to move, or to persuade." [11] We have in Campbell, then, one of the very few rhetorical theorists whose conception of rhetoric is not theoretically confined to persuasive discourse, and even Campbell makes persuasion the center and overriding interest of his theory.

When we turn from the two rhetorical theorists who seem most likely to give serious attention to expository discourse and view the practice of contemporary professional critics, we find even more marked the tendency to identify works of rhetoric as persuasive discourses. The three volumes, *A History and Criticism of American Public Address*, contain no essays on speakers whose public discourses were predominantly expository rather than persuasive.[12] The critical essays appearing in the *Quarterly Journal of Speech* reveal the same hiatus. In the decade beginning with 1950, there were no studies of expository speakers in that journal, no studies even of rhetorical situations where expository discourse could be expected to predominate, such as the classroom, the scientific meeting, the occasion of the doctrinal sermon. Essays in rhetorical criticism focus on persuasive speakers or discourses, and the weight of the rhetorical tradition too falls in that direction. Consequently, we are obliged to conclude that the subject matter of rhetorical criticism is persuasive discourse.

---

[11] Campbell, *op. cit.*, p. 222.
[12] William Norwood Brigance, ed., vols. I & II (New York, 1943); and Marie Kathryn Hochmuth, ed., vol. III, *A History and Criticism of American Public Address* (New York, 1955).

I. A. Richards has suggested a reason for the exclusive association of rhetoric with persuasive discourse in observing that ". . . neutral exposition is a very special limited use of language, comparatively a late development . . ." [13] Whatever the reason, the association exists, and if we are to survey accurately the practice of rhetorical criticism, we must accept it as a fact.

Of course, it is important to be clear about how rhetorical discourse is to be persuasive. Persuasive in this sense refers to intent, not necessarily to accomplishment. Rhetorical discourses are those discourses, spoken or written, which aim to influence men. Whether a given discourse actually exerts an influence has no bearing on whether it is rhetorical.

At this point we must note some objections that may be raised to defining rhetorical discourses as discourses "which aim to influence men." The concepts of aim or intent or purpose are all peculiarly anthropomorphic, and one may object that, although men can be described as having aims, intentions, or purposes, it is only figurative to ascribe them to things, such as discourses. It is true that metaphors are extraordinarily dangerous and sometimes misleading in speculative writing inasmuch as they can jeopardize the precision of an objective description. Moreover, appearances are notoriously deceptive. What may appear to be a man's intentions can turn out to be mistaken. Men often blunder, or they dissemble; they say one thing and mean something else, and consequently to read the aim or purpose of a man in the text of his writing is to be susceptible to deception. As one author has put it: "Too often we look to the *message* (speech, manuscript, play, advertisement) in order to determine communicative purpose. *From a behaviorist's point of view, it is more useful to define purpose as the goal of a creator or receiver of a message, rather than as the property of the message itself.*" [14]

These objections have a measure of validity. It is perfectly

---

[13] I. A. Richards, *The Philosophy of Rhetoric* (New York, 1936), p. 40.

[14] David K. Berlo, *The Process of Communication* (New York, 1960), p. 10. Berlo's italics.

true that the critic, determining the purpose of a text from evidence the text itself provides, can be mistaken. There is a margin for error and for disagreement in this phase of criticism. The essential question, however, is not whether mistakes can be made in attributing aim or intent or purpose to a text, but whether these mistakes occur often enough to force a prudent man to abandon the attempt. Is there, in sum, any sense to finding the aim of a discourse in evidence that the discourse itself provides?

Our answer lies in a postulate that must be found at the foundation of any system of rhetorical criticism. That postulate is that there will be a correspondence among the intentions of a communicator, the characteristics of his discourse, and the reactions of his auditors to that discourse. This postulate is justified by the fact that to deny it is to deny the possibility of language, as we ordinarily understand that term.

If there is no correspondence between the intentions of a communicator and the characteristics of his discourse, then expression is impossible. We grant this relationship when, wanting to go to the left, we tell the taxi driver, "Turn left." We know that the phrase, "Turn left," will correspond to our intentions in expressing those intentions better than any other sounds we could make. If there is no correspondence between the characteristics of a discourse and the reactions of auditors to it, then communication is impossible. We commonly grant this relationship too when, having said, "Turn left," we expect the taxi driver to execute a certain, prescribed maneuver.

Undoubtedly there are occasions when parts of this correspondence break down. Perhaps a passenger will say, "Turn left," when he really wants to go to the right, but he is momentarily confused. Or perhaps the taxi driver will turn right after he has been instructed to turn left, for the same reason. The slap on the back from the used car salesman does not really express his affection, and we sometimes realize it. The friendly greeting from the politician during his campaign is not an invariable sign of his goodwill. Mistakes happen, deceptions occur; the system sometimes collapses. That is why we must grant a margin for error in the critical findings postulated on this correspondence. But the important point is that we do regard such breakdowns in the system as exceptional, and almost every waking moment of our lives is spent with faith in the postulate. It is this postulate that makes possible our definition of rhetorical discourse as discourse that aims to influence. We have every reason for seeking the aims or purposes of a discourse, because we know that in the great majority of cases the aims and purposes of the communicator will be expressed, through conventional tokens, in his discourse. And as for the minority of cases in which the communicator's aims are obscured or disguised by his discourse, we have even learned to be alert to the circumstances in which we might be misled. Such sophistication is, indeed, a condition of survival in the twentieth century. We can see, then, that attributing a purpose or an aim to a discourse refers to no more than the expectation that the aims of a man will display their symptoms in what he says and how he says it.

While the discourse itself is the most usual source for evidence of intent, it is not the only possible source. We may encounter a discourse in which we find no evidence of persuasive intent, but we discover that the author of the discourse intended to persuade nonetheless. The evidence may be the author's own testimony, or the testimony of someone who knew his mind, or some aspect of the situation in which the discourse appeared that made persuasive intent mandatory. In those cases too we must regard the discourse as rhetorical because it has met the terms of the definition. We have discovered persuasive intent, and from this discovery we must regard the discourse as a fitting subject for rhetorical criticism, regardless of what nonrhetorical characteristics it may display.

The subject matter of rhetorical criticism, then, is usually taken to be discourse that aims to influence men. And what of its practice? The methods of rhetorical criticism, although they are embodied in an ever-growing literature, are neither so numerous nor so variegated as to be beyond reckoning. Preliminary to such reckoning we must note that not every commentary on a rhetorical discourse is a critique. Rhetorical discourses can be culled for many purposes other than understanding how they work, which is the task of criticism. The political reporter may examine the deliberative address for indications of future policy; the biographer may look for clues to a cast of mind and an inner life; the poetaster may read the oration for its passages of fire; the pilgrim may search the sermon for a faith. These are legitimate preoccupations, and there are more like them; but they are not criticism. They are not disinterested enough to be criticism. Criticism has no relationship with its subject other than to account for how that subject works; it demands nothing but full disclosure. That is an ideal, of course. In fact we do have critical essays that seek for more than how their subjects work, but insofar as the critic's motives are not disinterested, his criticism will be tainted. The standard of disinterested objectivity in criticism has stood too long and been too widely accepted to require further elaboration here.

Arnold, in his survey of rhetoric in the United States since 1900, finds virtually no systematic rhetorical criticism in this country prior to 1920.[15] Even that date is too early to mark the beginning of criticism of any sophistication, for, as Arnold remarks, ". . . the early attempts at critically appraising rhetorical practice were often crude and incomplete." [16] It is only in recent years that a set of practices associated with rhetorical criticism has evolved in this country and has become sufficiently stable to reward examination. Three distinct approaches to the practices of rhetorical criticism can be identified among the published critical writings in this country, with one of these three commanding by far the greatest allegiance among professional critics. They are (1) the movement study, in which the critic

---

[15] Carroll C. Arnold, "Rhetoric in America Since 1900," *Re-Establishing the Speech Profession. The First Fifty Years,* ed. Robert T. Oliver and Marvin G. Bauer (n.p., 1959), p. 5.

[16] *Ibid.*

focuses on the total dispute over a single program or policy, from the genesis of persuasion on the issue to the time when public discussion of it finally ends; (2) the psychological study, in which the critic traces the patterns of influence between a rhetor's inner life and his rhetorical activities; and (3) the neo-Aristotelian study, in which the critic applies to rhetorical discourse canons derived from classical rhetoric, particularly the *Rhetoric* of Aristotle. It is this last approach that is the most popular. It has, moreover, influenced the other two approaches without being much influenced by them in published criticism.

THE MOVEMENT STUDY

The movement study has received a brief theoretical statement by Griffin in which, having sketched the characteristic development of persuasive movements, he provides advice to the critic.

. . . the student will note the crystallization of fundamental issues, the successive emergence of argument, appeal, counter-argument and counter-appeal, and the sanctions invoked by rhetoricians of both sides; he will note, by a process of imaginative re-living in the age, by an analysis of consequences, the persuasive techniques which were effective and those which were ineffective; and he will note a time, very likely, when invention runs dry, when both aggressor and defendant rhetoricians tend to repeat their stock of argument and appeal. . . . He may note the development of organizations designed to facilitate the dissemination of argument, such as the lecture bureau, the committee of correspondence, and the political party. Finally, as he reads, the student will note the increasing circulation and the ultimate extent of the appeal; the development of audiences; and as the movement spreads, the geographical and social stratification of these audiences.[17]

---

[17] Leland M. Griffin, "The Rhetoric of Historical Movements," *Quarterly Journal of Speech*, XXXVIII (April 1952), pp. 186–187.

Griffin's own study of the antimasonic movement of the early nineteenth century illustrates the application of these techniques.[18] They are techniques fashioned for the analysis of argument on a large scale, for widening the scope of the rhetorical critic from the individual performance to the sweep of a persuasive campaign. And to characterize these techniques in this way is to reveal their limits as well as their applicability, for it is precisely the subject matter of criticism rather than its practice that the movement study affects. The implied distinction should not be pushed too far, of course. Subject matter and practice are interdependent—or at least ought to be—and a shift in one will almost always result in an alteration of the other, but insofar as we can reasonably distinguish between the two, it is the subject matter of criticism which is more affected by the movement study. In terms of critical practice, Griffin's recommendation is that of historical relativism.

> . . . the critic must judge the discourse in terms of the theories of rhetoric and public opinion indigenous to the times. This principle means that the critic will operate within the climate of theory of rhetoric and public opinion in which the speakers and writers he judges were reared, and in which they practiced; in other words, that he will measure practice in terms of the theories available, not to himself, but to the speakers and writers whom he judges. The principle means that the student of an early nineteenth-century movement will ground his judgments in the theories of Blair and Campbell; that the critic of a movement occurring within the last thirty years, on the other hand, will operate within the theoretical atmosphere created by latter-day rhetoricians, that he will acknowledge the presence of the propagandist, and the various devices of propaganda, in the theoretical atmosphere of the times.[19]

---

[18] Leland M. Griffin, "The Rhetorical Structure of the Antimasonic Movement," *The Rhetorical Idiom. Essays in Rhetoric, Oratory, Language, and Drama,* ed. Donald C. Bryant (Ithaca, N.Y., 1958).

[19] Griffin, *op. cit., Quarterly Journal of Speech,* XXXVIII (April 1952), p. 187.

For many purposes there can be no quarrel with Griffin's historically relative frame of critical reference. For critics to approach the study of movements in terms of the rhetorical theories affecting the movements themselves could not fail to illuminate the history of rhetorical practice. It is, then, to the rhetorical historian that Griffin offers the greatest promise. However, another hope of Griffin's seems more doubtful of fulfillment by the movement study: "From the identification of a number of rhetorical patterns, we may discover the various configurations of public discussion, whether rhetorical patterns repeat themselves when like movements occur in the intervals of time, whether a consistent set of forms may be said to exist." [20]

It does seem that, for an accumulation of movement studies to reveal recurring "rhetorical patterns," the studies must have seen the patterns in somewhat the same way. Different rhetorical historians, investigating different periods of rhetorical history, must at least share the same concept of "pattern," the same sense of "form," before their findings can be correlative. What relationship can there be between a Ciceronian critique of a persuasive movement in Roman history and a Campbellian critique of a persuasive movement in nineteenth-century America? Only so much relationship as there is between Cicero and Campbell. Insofar as Ciceronian theory and Campbellian theory record rhetorical activity in similar ways, the two critiques could, indeed, discern patterns. But insofar as Cicero and Campbell are dissimilar, studies based upon them would be incommensurable, would not note recurrent "configurations of public discussion," because each would have its own view of what constitutes a configuration.

There is one other difficulty, too, in Griffin's suggestions concerning critical practice in the movement study. It is that if one appraises a historical movement in terms "indigenous to the times," one would be voluntarily sacrificing one of the distinct advantages of historical perspective, and without a compensa-

---

[20] *Ibid.*, p. 188.

tory gain. To demonstrate, for example, as Howell does, that the argumentation of the Declaration of Independence was influenced by the rhetoric-logical theory of William Duncan is to perform a vital task of historical reconstruction; [21] but to appraise the Declaration in terms of Duncan's theory would be to forego all that we have learned since Duncan's time. It would be for the contemporaneous critic to abandon his own theory of rhetoric for Duncan's; but why would the contemporaneous critic have a theory at all if he did not believe it to be superior to Duncan's? We can well question Griffin's suggestions on critical practice if, as it seems, those suggestions would sometimes compel us to adopt inferior theories to guide our criticism.

These reservations concerning Griffin's theoretical position in no way alter the value we must accord that position. In suggesting a reconstitution of the subject matter of rhetorical criticism from the individual speaker or the individual speech to the persuasive movement, Griffin has opened a new and exciting prospect to rhetorical criticism. His own study of the antimasonic movement is a distinguished effort that highly recommends the mode. Yet, few movement studies in rhetoric have been published besides Griffin's.[22] Certainly there is as yet no cogent and reasonably uniform methodology for the movement study beyond Griffin's suggestion of historical relativism, and it is exactly in the area of methodology that Griffin seems least satisfactory.

THE PSYCHOLOGICAL STUDY

The rhetorical critique employing a psychological approach has received no formal methodological statement, but this approach is well illustrated by Maloney's essay on Clarence Dar-

---

[21] Wilbur Samuel Howell, "The Declaration of Independence and Eighteenth-Century Logic," *The William and Mary Quarterly*, 3rd ser., XVIII (October 1961), pp. 463–84.

[22] The *Quarterly Journal of Speech* has published only two in the last decade: E. James Lennon, "The Pro-Northern Movement in England, 1861–

row.[23] After arguing that his subject cannot be approached in a conventional manner, Maloney presents his hypothesis that Darrow's rhetorical career is to be accounted for mythically.

> We must now inquire briefly into the general structure of the Darrow myth. When Darrow, in defending himself against a charge of bribery before a Los Angeles jury in 1912, said, "I have stood for the weak and the poor. I have stood for the men who toil," he suggested the nature of the fable. It was as a defender of the underdog, a devil's advocate, a man who stood perpetually opposed to the great and powerful of the earth, that he became known. . . . The twin strands of aggressiveness and insecurity interweave in the pattern of American attitudes; and it is the major function of the "underdog" myth to rationalize and reconcile the two. Thus, an alien, a workingman, a Negro, following Darrow's triumphs, could see himself, in Darrow, triumphant over the forces that pressed him in, saving the unjustly doomed victim from the hangman, speaking out for freedom and justice; and at the same time might know himself the innocent victim, saved against all expectation from his enemies.[24]

Next Maloney considers the psychological influences in Darrow's early life, and finds in them the sources of Darrow's morbid fear of death, a fear which, Maloney argues, motivated many of Darrow's rhetorical transactions. The study then proceeds to sections that chart the temper of Darrow's times, trace the development of his career, and consider his use of persuasive technique. Finally, there is a longer section on Darrow's philosophical conclusions.

Maloney's is an extraordinary study. It is sensitively conceived and written in a style that is exactly suited to its subject. The

---

1865," XLI (February 1955), pp. 27–37; and W. David Lewis, "Three Religious Orators and the Chartist Movement," XLIII (February 1957), pp. 62–68. In the same period, *Speech Monographs* has only one: Eugene E. White, "The Protasis of the Great Awakening in New England," XXI (March 1954), pp. 10–20.

[23] Hochmuth, *op. cit.*, III, pp. 262–312.

[24] From *A History and Criticism of American Public Address*, ed. by Marie Kathryn Hochmuth (New York, 1955), vol. III, p. 266.

critic is less interested in Darrow's rhetorical performances than in Darrow as a creature of his times and a product of his environment, but the broader interest still illuminates the rhetorical activities. This interest leads Maloney to draw his analytic techniques from anthropology and psychoanalysis. His approach to the career of Darrow corresponds to Darrow's own approach to forensic situations. As Darrow's recurrent strategy in forensic pleading was to substitute a sociopsychological vocabulary for the standard legal-moral vocabulary of the courtroom, so Maloney's critical strategy is to apply a sociopsychological vocabulary to Darrow instead of the standard vocabulary of the critical essay. Maloney has written a "defense" of Darrow.

The critic's one lapse from his otherwise sustained psychological analysis—in the section on Darrow's persuasive techniques [25]—reveals, perhaps, the pristine state of this whole approach to rhetorical criticism. In this section, the critic appraises Darrow's speaking in the categories of logical proof, pathetic proof, and, though not called so in the essay, ethos. These categories, together with the isolation of a recurrent pattern of argument in Darrow's speeches, notes on Darrow's methods of selecting jurymen, and observations on Darrow's personal appearance do not constitute an entirely satisfactory accounting for the social symbol that Darrow became through his discourse. We need not seek far for the reason; we can sense it in the abrupt shift in tone when Maloney approaches the subject of rhetorical techniques. A method for the psychological examination of rhetorical discourse was simply not available to the critic and so, though he wrote a notably successful account of the genesis and social impact of Darrow's career, the character and power of Darrow's discourse is not so well explained.

Psychological criticism, it seems, can be quite fruitful in revealing the forces engendering a discourse, but when the discourse in its turn becomes an influential force, the resources of psychological criticism are strained to account for it. The psychological critic can, as in Maloney's essay on Darrow, disclose

---

[25] *Ibid.*, pp. 295–300.

the causal links between the rhetor and his discourse, and he can describe the way in which the discourse functions in its social setting, but his methodology does not equip him for explaining how that particular discourse came to function in that way. He is, in sum, prepared to deal with the discourse-as-symptom, but he is less able to deal with the discourse-as-communication.

There is, moreover, a danger of excessive gullibility in psychological criticism, a disposition to equate too simply and readily the author and his work. We can see the danger manifested even in the efforts of Kenneth Burke, who has written some of our subtlest psychological criticism. Here is Burke writing on T. S. Eliot's play, *Murder in the Cathedral:*

> A work on Thomas the Saint, by Thomas the Poet, the Saint Louis boy who was too good for Saint Louis (why shouldn't he be!). Concerned with the royal road to God.
>
> Stages: The author leaves the old locale behind to go in search of its antithesis. He will abandon the inelegancies of Missouri for the elegancies of upper-class England. By antithesis, he builds up a concept of elegance—and then he goes in search of it *geographically*. He tries to find a place here-and-now that will give sufficient bodily substance to the structure of his imagination. For a time he thinks he has found it in England. But eventually it occurs to him that England is moving towards Saint Louis. Life becomes a waste land at the thought. England is not elegant enough. And eventually the poet meditates upon God, the only symbol elegant enough. But.
>
> Being a profound and imaginative man, being perhaps our most accomplished poet, Eliot knows very well that there is no slogan: *per elegantiam ad astra.* He questions the validity of his way. He knows that he must get to God by humbleness, so he must "transcend" his elegance, building atop it a new structure of humility. The God of elegance being the negation of Saint Louis, he must round out his development by "negating the negation." "Murder in the Cathedral" is the symbolic solution of this problem in spiritual tactics.[26]

---

[26] Kenneth Burke, *Attitudes Toward History,* vol. I (New York, 1937), pp. 109–10.

No doubt this is lively and amusing writing, even if it is, un-typical of Burke, unkind; but one can question how much it really reveals about either *Murder in the Cathedral* or T. S. Eliot. We can doubt, as a psychologist probably would, that a quest for "elegance" is ever in itself a very profound motive to action, and we can suspect that such a quest, if it exists in a particular case, is never any but the most superficial expression of motive. More broadly, we can doubt that Eliot's inner life bore quite so simple a relationship to his play as Burke alleges. We are certainly entitled to doubt, since Burke has not cited evidence for his interpretation.

We are compelled to believe in the existence of relation-ships between a man's deepest motives and his discourses. Such a conviction is bound up with the very ways we have of talking about human motives. The mystery lies in the identification of those characteristics of discourse which reveal motive, for we know that motive only rarely receives a full and direct expres-sion. Usually, the motives of a man are transmuted in their linguistic expression; they are symbolized in his discourse rather than openly reported. Our difficulty, as critics, is not only that we do not fully understand how and when and why these trans-mutations occur, but also that these transmutations may not even follow stable and regular patterns. Thus, for example, a patient of Freud's in the early part of this century might so con-sistently dream and write and talk of arrows as phallic symbols that Freud, with his ingenious capacity for translation, is able to discern the motivational meaning of the symbol. Freud then publishes his findings on this patient and notes that, in the cases of other patients too, arrows are phallic symbols, so that the arrow seems to have a general symbolic value. But then—and here is where the critic is invited to disaster—someone who speaks or writes reads Freud and learns that he can disguise his true motives by writing and speaking of arrows, for he knows that his auditors, themselves having been influenced by Freud, will interpret arrow to mean phallus and not, as it means to him, something entirely different. In short, just as Freud discovered that a person who has mastered ordinary language can use it to conceal his motives, so a person who has mastered Freudian vocabulary can use it too to conceal his motives. The possibilities of deception, deliberate or unconscious, seem endless, and consequently the problems presented the psychological critic seem insoluble. Our conclusion should assuredly not be that psychological criticism must be forever abandoned; but we are obliged to approach this enterprise with the most extreme caution. The methodology of psychological criticism is in a decidedly primitive state, and freighted with exceedingly taxing philosophical problems. In the psychological study of rhetorical discourse, as in the case of the movement study, we have little more than a promising beginning. With Maloney's essay on Darrow, the promise is high, but there is clearly no system of analysis or body of techniques available to the critic for the reliable psychological examination of argumentative strategies or discursive texture.

THE NEO-ARISTOTELIAN STUDY

By far the dominant mode of rhetorical criticism of the present century in the United States has been neo-Aristotelianism. Of the forty essays on individual speakers included in the three volumes of A History and Criticism of American Public Address, fifteen of the studies employ techniques of criticism derived from Aristotle's Rhetoric.[27] The proportion of neo-Aristotelian

---

[27] Brigance and Hochmuth, op. cit. The neo-Aristotelian essays are Orville Hitchcock, "Jonathan Edwards," I, pp. 213–237; Roy C. McCall, "Theodore Parker," I, pp. 238–264; Wayland Maxfield Parrish and Alfred Dwight Huston, "Robert G. Ingersoll," I, pp. 363–386; Karl R. Wallace, "Booker T. Washington," I, pp. 407–433; John W. Black, "Rufus Choate," I, pp. 434–458; Charles A. Fritz, "Edwin A. Alderman," II, pp. 540–556; Walter B. Emery, "Samuel Gompers," II, pp. 557–579; Ernest J. Wrage, "Henry Clay," II, pp. 603–638; Herbert L. Curry, "John C. Calhoun," II, pp. 639–664; R. Elaine Pagel and Carl Dallinger, "Charles Sumner," II, pp. 751–776; Carroll P. Lahman, "Robert M. LaFollete," II, pp. 942–967; Dayton David McKean, "Woodrow Wilson," II, pp. 968–992; Bower Aly, "Alexander Hamilton," III, pp. 24–51; Richard Murphy, "Theodore Roosevelt," III, pp. 313–364; Earnest Brandenburg and Waldo W. Braden, "Franklin Delano Roosevelt," III, pp. 458–530.

essays becomes even more striking when we note that of the twenty-five essays that remain unaccounted for, some employ only one or two of Aristotle's canons to serve for the entire critical apparatus,[28] some are biographical essays which make little attempt at critical interpretation or appraisal,[29] and some are appreciations, eulogies, or of dubious character.[30] Only eight of the essays attempt an examination and appraisal of rhetorical discourses by the employment of techniques which are singular or which represent unconventional interpretations or applications of traditional rhetoric.[31] It is further noteworthy that the editor of the first two volumes of these studies takes Aristotelian rhetoric as his point of departure in commenting upon the essays,[32] and that the editor of the third volume recommends the Aristotelian definition of rhetoric in her introductory essay,[33]

---

[28] *Ibid.*, Lester Thonssen, "William M. Evarts," I, pp. 483–500; Louis M. Eich, "Charles W. Eliot," II, pp. 526–539; Forest L. Whan, "Stephen A. Douglas," II, pp. 777–827; Mildred Freburg Berry, "Abraham Lincoln: His Development in the Skills of the Platform," II, pp. 828–858; Robert D. Clark, "Harry Emerson Fosdick," III, pp. 411–457.

[29] *Ibid.*, Willard Hayes Yeager, "Wendell Phillips," I, pp. 329–362; Marvin G. Bauer, "Henry W. Grady," I, pp. 387–406; Louis A. Mallory, "Patrick Henry," II, pp. 580–602; Earl W. Wiley, "Abraham Lincoln: His Emergence as the Voice of the People," II, pp. 859–877; Henry G. Roberts, "James G. Blaine," II, pp. 878–890; Dallas C. Dickey and Donald C. Streeter, "Lucius Q. C. Lamar," III, pp. 175–221.

[30] *Ibid.*, Lionel Crocker, "Henry Ward Beecher," I, pp. 265–293; Rexford S. Mitchell, "William L. Yancy," II, pp. 734–750; Myron G. Phillips, "William Jennings Bryan," II, pp. 891–918; Herold Truslow Ross, "Albert J. Beveridge," II, pp. 919–941; Doris Yoakam Twichell, "Susan B. Anthony," III, pp. 97–132; Robert B. Huber, "Dwight L. Moody," III, pp. 222–261.

[31] *Ibid.*, Marie Hochmuth and Norman Mattis, "Phillips Brooks," I, pp. 294–328; William Norwood Brigance, "Jeremiah S. Black," I, pp. 459–482; Herbert A. Wichelns, "Ralph Waldo Emerson," II, pp. 501–525; Wilbur Samuel Howell and Hoyt Hopewell Hudson, "Daniel Webster," II, pp. 665–733; Norman W. Mattis, "Thomas Hart Benton," III, pp. 52–96; Carroll C. Arnold, "George William Curtis," III, pp. 133–174; Martin Maloney, "Clarence Darrow," III, pp. 262–312; A. E. Whitehead, "William E. Borah," III, pp. 365–410.

[32] *Ibid.*, William Norwood Brigance, "Preface," I, p. x.

[33] *Ibid.*, Marie Kathryn Hochmuth, "The Criticism of Rhetoric," III, pp. 4 and 8.

and borrows several of the Aristotelian categories in the critical system she delineates.[34]

Hitchcock's essay on Jonathan Edwards will serve as a clear example of neo-Aristotelian criticism.[35] After arguing that Edwards' rhetorical biography has been neglected and is a needful study, Hitchcock has brief sections on the ethos of colonial Northampton and on Edwards' training and intellectual development. Then there follows the main critical section of the essay. In this critique Hitchcock first enumerates the "doctrines which Edwards preached." [36] He finds eight of them, and is able to convey each of the eight in a single sentence. Hitchcock then proceeds to his topics of criticism. First is organization: "Jonathan Edwards's sermons are highly organized . . . Each is divided broadly into four large sections; the thesis is carefully stated; the discussion is developed in three or four main points; these main points are arranged according to a definite system (the order is usually logical or topical); and each tends to establish the principal thesis; the transitions from one idea to another are smoothly and easily made; frequent summaries occur." [37]

Under the heading "Organization" Hitchcock goes on to discuss the character of Edwards' introductions and conclusions, after having made some additional observations on Edwards' general practices in arranging discourse.

"Types of Proof" is the next topic. "Edwards's argumentative method" is divided into inductive and deductive methods.[38] We are told that "categorical, hypothetical, and disjunctive enthymemes appear in every sermon," [39] that "argument from authority greatly predominates," [40] and that "argument by explanation also becomes an important instrument of proof." [41]

---

[34] *Ibid.*, passim.
[35] *Ibid.*, I, pp. 213–237.
[36] *Ibid.*, I, p. 220.
[37] *Ibid.*, I, p. 222.
[38] *Ibid.*, I, p. 223.
[39] *Ibid.*, I, p. 224.
[40] *Ibid.*
[41] *Ibid.*, I, p. 225.

Next Hitchcock examines the "emotional approach": "While Edwards uses a great many pathetic arguments, these appeals are, in general, subordinated to the logical elements." [42] "The principal appeals are to fear, shame, desire for happiness, security, and pride. Gratitude, common sense, emulation, greed, and courage receive less emphasis. In appealing to fear, Edwards frequently refers to hell." [43]

"Ethical proof" is examined: "Edwards . . . presented a strong ethical argument. His life was exemplary; he followed a strict moral code; his friends and neighbors thought well of him." [44]

Then style:

> Edwards wrote his sermons in a precise, plain, exact style. Nothing of fine writing or of excessive display creeps into his text. Nor are there classical allusions or other learned references. The language is the language of the audience; it is constantly toned down to the listeners' level. The analogies and comparisons are of an everyday type, apt and exact, yet often the commonest form. The quotations are Biblical and are cited with a matter-of-factness that appealed to the most unlearned listener. Even Edwards's own language has a Biblical flavor. His style can best be described as common and precise, patterned after that of the Scriptures. [45]

After further considerations of "style," Hitchcock concludes with a short section on "methods of preparation and delivery" and one on "effect." In the latter section, Hitchcock is concerned with the effects of Edwards' sermons on his immediate audience.

Enough of Hitchcock's essay has been quoted to disclose his particular merits and defects as a critic. What is important here is the general method of criticism being employed, irrespective

---

[42] *Ibid.*, I, p. 227.
[43] *Ibid.*, I, p. 227.
[44] *Ibid.*, I, p. 230.
[45] *Ibid.*

of the skill of its particular applications. The general method is what has been designated *neo-Aristotelianism*, and Hitchcock's essay is an especially clear example of it because of the literalness with which the method is applied in this essay and the clarity with which its canons of criticism are invoked.

The primary and identifying ideas of neo-Aristotelianism that we can find recurring in the critical essays of this school are the classification of rhetorical discourses into forensic, deliberative, and epideictic; the classification of "proofs" or "means of persuasion" into logical, pathetic, and ethical; the assessment of discourse in the categories of invention, arrangement, delivery, and style; and the evaluation of rhetorical discourse in terms of its effects on its immediate audience. Each of these ideas is prominent in the Hitchcock essay except for the first. In the case of the tripartite typology of rhetorical discourses, Hitchcock was dealing with a genre—the sermon—that is post-Aristotelian and, consequently, is not easily reconciled with the traditional typology; but even in dealing with this special genre, Hitchcock scrupulously adheres to the conventions of neo-Aristotelianism.

The practice of neo-Aristotelian criticism has received formal statement in an essay first published in 1925. Wichelns' program for rhetorical criticism appeared in a significant paragraph.

Rhetorical criticism is necessarily analytic. The scheme of a rhetorical study includes the element of the speaker's personality as a conditioning factor; it includes also the public character of the man—not what he was, but what he was thought to be. It requires a description of the speaker's audience, and of the leading ideas with which he plied his hearers—his topics, the motives to which he appealed, the nature of the proofs he offered. These will reveal his own judgment of human nature in his audiences, and also his judgment on the questions which he discussed. Attention must be paid, too, to the relation of the surviving texts to what was actually uttered: in case the nature of the changes is known, there may be occasion to consider adaptation to two audiences—that which heard and that which read. Nor can rhetorical criticism omit the speaker's mode of arrangement and his mode of expression, nor his habit of preparation and his manner of delivery from the platform; though the last two are perhaps less significant. "Style"—in the sense which corresponds to diction and sentence movement—must receive attention, but only as one among various means that secure for the speaker ready access to the minds of his auditors. Finally, the effect of the discourse on its immediate hearers is not to be ignored, either in the testimony of witnesses, nor in the record of events. And throughout such a study one must conceive of the public man as influencing the men of his own times by the power of his discourse.[46]

Bryant's judgment—that this essay "set the pattern and determined the direction of rhetorical criticism for more than a quarter of a century and has had a greater and more continuous influence upon the development of the scholarship of rhetoric and public address than any other single work published in this century" [47]—suggests that one of the main sources of neo-Aristotelianism may lie in the influence of Wichelns' program of 1925. The elements of analysis recommended in the quoted paragraph could be a compendium of the topics of Aristotle or Cicero: ". . . the public character of the man . . . his topics, the motives to which he appealed, the nature of the proofs he offered . . . the speaker's mode of arrangement and his mode of expression . . . his manner of delivery from the platform . . . diction and sentence movement . . . the effect of the discourse on its immediate hearers."

The uses to which Aristotle can be interpreted as having put these topics is not the present issue. What is pertinent in clarifying neo-Aristotelianism is the fact that these are subjects for discussion in the neo-Aristotelian essay, just as they were subjects for discussion in the *Rhetoric*. Even in its most faithful

---

[46] Herbert A. Wichelns, "The Literary Criticism of Oratory," *The Rhetorical Idiom. Essays in Rhetoric, Oratory, Language, and Drama*, ed. Donald C. Bryant (Ithaca, N.Y., 1958), pp. 38–39.

[47] Donald C. Bryant, ed., *The Rhetorical Idiom. Essays in Rhetoric, Oratory, Language, and Drama* (Ithaca, N.Y., 1958), p. 5.

executions, neo-Aristotelian criticism cannot be certain of serving the purposes of Aristotle's *Rhetoric*. Aristotle has left us
with no substantial body of criticism, and we can only conjecture
the extent to which, had Aristotle left any, his critical writing
would adhere to the principles of the *Rhetoric* or would strictly
subordinate rhetorical criticism to logical analysis and political
commentary. There may be little that the neo-Aristotelians have
in common with Aristotle besides some recurrent topics of discussion and a vaguely derivative view of rhetorical discourse;
but even so, these topics and this view may serve to define neo-
Aristotelianism.

The view itself must be found behind neo-Aristotelian critiques rather than explicitly stated in them. It is a view which
the neo-Aristotelian essays share. The first element of this view
is the comprehension of the rhetorical discourse as tactically designed to achieve certain results with a specific audience on a
specific occasion. Of the fifteen neo-Aristotelian essays in *A History and Criticism of American Public Address*, only two undertake an appraisal of rhetorical discourse in terms other than its
effect on an immediate audience.[48] There is little disposition
among neo-Aristotelian critics to comprehend the discourse in a
larger context, to see it, as for example the movement study
would, as part of a historical process of argument. To the neo-
Aristotelian, the discourse is discrete and its relevant effects are
immediate.[49]

---

[48] The two exceptions are Bower Aly, "Alexander Hamilton," III, pp. 24–
51; and Richard Murphy, "Theodore Roosevelt," II, pp. 313–364. Aly
attempts to determine Hamilton's "place in the history of oratory" (pp.
49–50); Murphy attempts an assessment of Roosevelt's permanent value
as an orator as well as his effectiveness (pp. 359–360).

[49] In this connection, it is instructive to note the series of experimental
studies conducted by Hovland and his associates at Yale University:
Carl I. Hovland, Irving L. Janis, and Harold H. Kelley, *Communication
and Persuasion* (New Haven, 1953); Carl I. Hovland (ed.), *The Order
of Presentation in Persuasion* (New Haven, 1957); Carl I. Hovland and
Irving L. Janis (ed.), *Personality and Persuasibility* (New Haven, 1959).
Insofar as the social scientists focus on discourses rather than on audience
reactions to them, they display the same interest as neo-Aristotelian critics
in the discreteness of the discourse, and in its immediate effects. Cf.

Another element of the view of rhetorical discourse sustained in neo-Aristotelianism is the close relationship between rhetoric and logic. Perhaps the most striking result of this relationship is the tendency of neo-Aristotelian critics to concentrate on discourses that approach logical demonstration and to eschew the explication of discourses that do not have a demonstrative form. All the subjects of neo-Aristotelian essays in A *History and Criticism of American Public Address* are orators in the genteel tradition. Most of them are of the nineteenth century. The few orators treated in these volumes whose discourses are ill-suited to logical analysis—Patrick Henry, Dwight L. Moody, perhaps William Jennings Bryan—are not subjected to neo-Aristotelian criticism.

Following also from the close relationship between rhetoric and logic, which seems to characterize neo-Aristotelianism, is the tendency to assume the rationality of audiences. The very terms argument and proof are borrowed from logic and are repeatedly employed by neo-Aristotelian critics. Audiences are conceived of as responsive to arguments and proofs; and even "emotional appeals," which appears to be the rubric for persuasive discourse not susceptible to logical explanation, are often conceived of as a type of proof.

In charting the pattern of influence that flows through the rhetorical transaction, the neo-Aristotelian critic typically sees

---

Communication and Persuasion, pp. 56–130; and all of *The Order of Presentation in Persuasion*. Moreover, they have the same tendency as neo-Aristotelian critics to fragment the discourse and to investigate its constituents as independent variables. The approach of the Hovland group, of course, is necessitated by the technical demands of the experimental method rather than by a commitment to a critical system; however, the approaches to the rhetorical discourse are sufficiently similar so that the data unearthed by the Yale investigators could, with a minimum of mediation, directly inform neo-Aristotelianism.

The Yale studies of audiences, *Communication and Persuasion*, pp. 134–265, and all of *Personality and Persuasibility*, are in a different category. Enlisting the resources of psychology for the measurement of personality, learning, and intelligence, and relating these factors to persuasibility, these investigations have relevance to any conceivable system of rhetorical criticism and, indeed, are in the area in which rhetorical criticism must rely heavily on the findings of the social sciences.

only one direction of movement: the background, training, interests, and aims of the rhetor influence his discourse, which in turn influences the audience. The neo-Aristotelians ignore the impact of the discourse on rhetorical conventions, its capacity for disposing an audience to expect certain ways of arguing and certain kinds of justifications in later discourses that they encounter, even on different subjects. Similarly, the neo-Aristotelian critics do not account for the influence of the discourse on its author: the future commitments it makes for him, rhetorically and ideologically; the choices it closes to him, rhetorically and ideologically; the public image it portrays to which he must adjust.

Our characterization of neo-Aristotelianism has been only preliminary. Because this approach to rhetorical criticism has been so dominant as to have come, in many minds, to be identified as the whole of rhetorical criticism, the pages to follow will afford it fuller treatment. It may serve as a summary statement of this preliminary definition to note again the treatment rhetorical discourse receives from each of the three practices of criticism that have been reviewed: the movement study treats of discourse as an element in a complex of historical forces shaping public opinion and public policy; the psychological study regards the rhetorical discourse as a symptom or consequence of the personal history of the rhetor, and as an element in a social configuration; neo-Aristotelianism treats rhetorical discourses as discrete communications in specific contexts, designed for specific purposes.

Our next task must be to look even more carefully at the generic nature of criticism and, with this perspective, to determine more exactly how—and if—neo-Aristotelianism works.

CHAPTER III

Rhetoric and
General Criticism

IN CONSIDERING the generic functions of criticism, the aesthetician Theodore M. Greene analyzes criticism into three constituents: the historical, the re-creative, and the judicial.[1] Since Greene is referring to criticism in general rather than to criticism of any particular method or application, his analysis will serve as a useful point of departure for our examination of the dominant mode of rhetorical criticism, neo-Aristotelianism.

Greene notes, of the three constituents of criticism: "Each aspect relates itself to a corresponding aspect of the work of art itself—historical criticism, to the work's historical character and

---

[1] Theodore M. Greene, *The Arts and the Art of Criticism* (Princeton, N.J., 1947).

orientation; re-creative criticism, to its unique artistic individuality; and judicial criticism, to its artistic value." [2]

> The special task of historical criticism is that of determining the nature and expressive intent of works of art in their historical context; . . . of re-creative criticism . . . that of apprehending imaginatively, through sensitive artistic response, what the artist has actually succeeded in expressing in a specific work of art; . . . of judicial criticism . . . that of estimating the value of a work of art in relation to other works of art and to other human values.[3]

Greene further emphasizes that ". . . these three aspects of criticism are in reality three complementary approaches to the work of art, and that each approach can be explored effectively only in conjunction with the other two." [4]

With Greene's analysis of general criticism before us, we can now inquire more deeply into the function of neo-Aristotelian criticism.

HISTORICAL CRITICISM

There is, among practicing critics, broad agreement on the nature of historical criticism as it is applied to works of rhetoric, at least of historical criticism in its preliminary stages. The authentication of texts and their interpretation in the light of biographical, social, and ideological evidence proceeds along lines prescribed by scholarly tradition. While there can be, and is, disagreement about particular historical interpretations and the weight to be given evidence, these disagreements rarely extend to questions of what a valid interpretation is or what constitutes evidence. Disputes arising in historical criticism almost invariably relate to specific judgments in historiography, and are to be resolved in terms of the specific data pertinent to those

---

[2] *Ibid.*, pp. 369f.
[3] *Ibid.*, p. 370.
[4] *Ibid.*

judgments. But the standards for performing a reconstruction of a work's context—discovering data, verifying them, and drawing inferences therefrom—do not vary in the application of historical criticism to different sorts of works. As one critic has put it in comparing rhetorical with literary criticism, ". . . methods and materials in literary history and critical scholarship apply likewise in oratory and rhetoric. Some modifications and adaptations, of course, are necessary; but we always have an overlapping so great that method in literary history is almost the same as in rhetorical history." [5]

While the standards and methods of preliminary historical criticism—the discovery of historical context—are not unique to neo-Aristotelianism, the application of these methods by neo-Aristotelian critics is shaped by the particular demands of their point of view. This shaping occurs in two important aspects of historical criticism: the relative importance of rhetorical history to the total critical process, and the selection of relevant historical data.

The discovery of historical context is especially important to the neo-Aristotelian critic of rhetorical discourse. It is vital for him to assess the discourse in a specific context because of his penchant for appraising the discourse as a response to a particular occasion. In this respect the neo-Aristotelian differs markedly from the critic of a fine art.

Handel's "Water Music" was composed, on commission, for a particular occasion, yet it stands as an object for criticism independent of that occasion. The music can be performed, appreciated, and evaluated without respect to the circumstances of its composition or its first performance. Similarly, Eliot wrote *Murder in the Cathedral*, on a specific commission, to commemorate an ecclesiastical anniversary; yet its performance,

---

[5] Donald C. Bryant, "Some Problems of Scope and Method in Rhetorical Scholarship," *Quarterly Journal of Speech*, XXIII (April 1937), p. 182. Bryant has more recently reaffirmed this position in "Rhetoric: Its Functions and Its Scope," *Quarterly Journal of Speech*, XXXIX (December 1953), p. 422.

its interpretation, and its appraisal can occur without regard to that occasion. But the neo-Aristotelian critic cannot interpret or evaluate Wendell Phillip's vindication of Lovejoy at will. The speech was so integrally a part of an occasion as to make some parts of it incomprehensible without reference to that occasion; so that a discovery of its context is requisite to interpreting it. And, for the neo-Aristotelian critic, this context is equally necessary to his appraisal of the speech since, as we have already remarked, he appraises the discourse in terms of its effects on a relatively immediate audience.

It is generally true that the work of rhetoric is fragmentary outside its environment; it functions only in a particular world. By contrast, the work of fine art is more self-sufficient and detached from any specific ambiance. This fact gives the discovery of context an enhanced importance in rhetorical criticism as compared to the criticism of fine arts. Of course, how broadly the rhetorical critic will interpret the term context depends on his objectives. As we have already noted, the neo-Aristotelian critics tend, on the whole, to take a restricted view of context, their tendency being to comprehend the rhetorical discourse as tactically designed to achieve certain results with a specific audience on a specific occasion.

Marie Hochmuth Nichols' essay on Lincoln's First Inaugural Address serves as a good example of this restricted view of context, not only because its pages of historical criticism are unusually thorough, but also because its scope is unusually explicit. Hochmuth's expression of her critical concern reveals a consciousness of Aristotelian canons.

> Unlike the historian, we are not concerned merely with the Inaugural as a force in the shaping of American culture; nor are we concerned with its enduring worth as literature. The Inaugural was a speech, "meant to be heard and intended to exert an influence of some kind on those who heard it," or those who read it. We must, therefore, be concerned with evaluating the Inaugural as a speech, a medium distinct from other media, and with methods peculiarly its own. We must be concerned with discover-

ing in this particular case "the available means of persuasion" and with evaluating their worth.[6]

The first quotation in the passage is from Parrish's essay, "The
Study of Speeches," which, as we shall subsequently see, is a
neo-Aristotelian statement, and the second quotation is, of
course, from the *Rhetoric* itself. At the very least we can infer
an affinity for neo-Aristotelianism in Hochmuth's selection of
her areas of concern, even if the whole of her very able essay
does not routinely adhere to the orthodoxies of any critical
school. What is striking in the passage is the critic's minimizing her concern for the First Inaugural "as a force in the shaping of American culture."

We have, first, Lincoln's repeated assertions in his debates
with Douglas that the opinions and sentiments of the people
were more important than the laws that governed them, that
these opinions and sentiments would, in fact, determine the
effectiveness of those laws. We have the argument of Edmund
Wilson, based mainly on Lincoln's address before the Young
Men's Lyceum of Springfield, Illinois in 1838, that even at that
early date Lincoln was already grooming himself to be a force
in American culture.[7] We have the argument of Richard Hofstadter that Lincoln consciously molded his discourses to the
end that they themselves would constitute a force in American
culture.[8] Finally, we have the argument of Harry V. Jaffa that
Lincoln's view of the "primary task of political leadership was
to maintain and strengthen the opinion" upon which certain
fundamental Constitutional guarantees rested.[9] We have, in
sum, some compelling reasons for suspecting that Lincoln's discourses were consciously designed to be strong and enduring

---

[6] Marie Hochmuth, "Lincoln's First Inaugural," Wayland Maxfield Parrish and Marie Hochmuth (ed.), *American Speeches* (New York, 1954),
p. 57.
[7] See Edmund Wilson, "Abraham Lincoln: The Union as Religious Mysti-
cism," *Eight Essays* (New York, 1954), pp. 181–202.
[8] See Richard Hofstadter, "Abraham Lincoln and the Self-Made Myth,"
The American Political Tradition and The Men Who Made It (New
York, 1948), pp. 92–134.
[9] Harry V. Jaffa, *Crisis of the House Divided: An Interpretation of the Issues in the Lincoln-Douglas Debates* (New York, 1959), p. 203.

forces shaping American culture, and that creating such discourses to serve such an objective was Lincoln's paramount objective. Whence, then, the critic's focus on the immediate audience and the immediate situation? Clearly, this focus is not dictated by the rhetor. It is, rather, the product of a critical assumption—one that is characteristic of neo-Aritotelianism.

It is true, and it must be acknowledged with some emphasis, that Hochmuth did not have available to her the interpretations of Wilson and Jaffa when she composed her own essay, although she did have available the same addresses of Lincoln on which these interpretations are based. The point here is to indicate how, in an essay of considerable merit, the neo-Aristotelian concept of context has worked to shape the view of a critic. Quite naturally, this concept affects the critic's selection of historical data in constructing the context. The Hochmuth essay contains a summary paragraph on the subject of relevant context.

What, then, was Lincoln's purpose? Clearly, he intended to take the occasion of the inauguration to declare the position of the Republican party in regard to the South, to announce his considered judgment in regard to the practical questions raised by the movement of secession, and, in all, to give what assurance he could of his personal integrity.[10]

In the remainder of her essay, the critic employs this interpretation of Lincoln's purpose as a ground for her appraisal of the speech.

There is no question of the accuracy of Hochmuth's statement of purpose. The statement is preceded by thirty-eight pages of scrupulous documentation in the critical essay. We should, however, note the scope of the statement, especially in the light of the subsequent interpretations of Wilson, Hofstadter, and Jaffa. The precise difference between Hochmuth's statement of purpose and that suggested by the other three critics is one of scope in selecting data. Influenced by neo-Aristotelianism, Hochmuth has selected data pertinent to the immediate audience of the First Inaugural and the specific occasion of its delivery. The other three critics, by contrast,

---

[10] Hochmuth, *op. cit.*, p. 59.

gather data taken from a wider range of American experience; Wilson even goes beyond the limits of peculiarly American experience to cull ideas from the psychology of religion and the nature of tragedy. Hochmuth's procedure precludes the scope of the other three; but any of the other three could very well include Hochmuth's statement of purpose were he to explicate the First Inaugural. What must be remarked is, first, the influence of neo-Aristotelianism in the critic's selection of data, and, second, the fact that there is no inevitability about this particular selection. The consideration of other historical data could lead to equally reasonable and perhaps richer statements of Lincoln's purpose.

Let us be reminded here that Greene assigns to historical criticism the task "of determining the nature and expressive intent of works of art in their historical context." The phrase "expressive intent" seems to refer to no more than what the artist intends to express in his work. It corresponds to Hochmuth's "purpose." Indeed, her very wording tends to confirm this correspondence: "What, then, was Lincoln's purpose? Clearly, he *intended* . . . etc." [11] What we may take as established is that the neo-Aristotelian critic can and often does make an effort to determine the "nature and expressive intent" of rhetorical discourse in its historical context, and that, consequently, the neo-Aristotelian critic is capable of fulfilling the historiographical task of generic criticism. At the same time, we must bear in mind that neo-Aristotelianism understands historical context in a particular and delimited way, and that this understanding, in turn, delimits and particularizes the range of expressive intents that neo-Aristotelianism would ascribe to a rhetorical discourse.

RE-CREATIVE CRITICISM

The function of re-creative criticism in neo-Aristotelianism is much less clear than that of historical criticism. The rendering

---

[11] My italics.

of re-creative criticism in the fine arts turns on the sensitivity and perceptiveness of the critic. This aspect of the total critical act makes the critic a participant rather than a detached observer, enabling him to comprehend the aesthetic experience in a sympathetic intuition of its object. Re-creation involves a reaction to the work of art *qua* art. It occurs when the critic is moved by the tragedy, amused by the farce, responds to the poem with just the shade of attitude that the poem can evoke. Re-creation involves a suspension of analytical objectivity in a surrender to the claims of the art object. Greene has more to say on the subject:

> Really to *re*-create a work of art is to apprehend the content which its author actually expressed in it, i.e., to interpret it correctly as a vehicle of communication. . . . Only man's artistic sensitivity can reveal what is and what is not a "work of art," and so, what does and what does not constitute the appropriate subject-matter of artistic and literary history. On the other hand, only that can be subjected to valid artistic appraisal which has been faithfully re-created. Appraisal cannot be based on rules or principles permitting of a purely mechanical application. We must "feel" what we would judge; our appraisal must be based upon an immediate artistic experience in the presence of the work of art itself.[12]

This part of Greene's analysis of general criticism is unsatisfying; unsatisfying because he does not demonstrate that re-creation is a part of criticism proper. If criticism is a body of writing containing the results of certain investigations into art objects, then re-creation does not seem so much a part of criticism as it does the psychological prerequisite to it. Of course, we are not obliged to treat Greene as if he were oracular. His examination of generic criticism is a convenient framework, and we need take it as no more. However, his concept of re-creative criticism, although it may be no part of criticism at all, does

12 Theodore M. Greene, *The Arts and The Art of Criticism* (Princeton, N.J., 1947), p. 371.

have the merit of focussing on the relationship between the critic and the object of his criticism, and in this respect it is a useful point of departure for our examination of neo-Aristotelianism.

The relationship between the neo-Aristotelian critic and the rhetorical discourse does seem decisively different from the relationship between the aesthetic critic and the art object. The object of the literary critic's interest, for example, is so constructed that there is a normative reaction to it. A poem can be read with varying degrees of adequacy, and the objective of re-creative criticism, in Greene's sense, would be to arrive at the poem's best possible reading.

One could respond to *Oedipus Rex* purely as a detective story, drawing no qualitative distinction (or only a slight one) between it and an ordinary mystery novel; but, of course, *Oedipus Rex* is much more than just a detective story, and we would regard an interpretation of it in such terms as evidence of the critic's imperceptiveness. There lies behind re-creative response, and the interpretation to which it gives rise, some standard of an ideal response and an ideal interpretation, and some criteria for knowing or finding out whether a given interpretation of a poem has been more or less satisfactory. The fact that neo-Aristotelianism does not warrant such a normative reaction to rhetorical discourse has made its version of re-creation a dubious enterprise—certainly quite different from what re-creation is in fine art.

Neo-Aristotelianism, which takes the relatively short-range intentions of the rhetor as given and then seeks to appraise the effects of the discourse against these intentions, does not yield a sanction for saying that one should have been persuaded by a speech. By contrast, we would have a presumption against the aesthetic sensitivity of the person who failed to respond to, say, *Macbeth*. Even for an auditor to mistake the intentions of a rhetorical discourse could not, in neo-Aristotelianism, be taken as a reflection on the auditor. More probably, such an error would suggest to the neo-Aristotelian critic a defect in the discourse that caused certain sorts of people to misinterpret it. But for a reader to attribute the wrong theme to a poem is taken generally as evidence that the reader has been inadequate.

Immanuel Kant illuminated the distinction relevant here when, in discussing beauty, he argued that it was of two kinds: "free beauty (*pulchritudo vaga*), or beauty which is merely dependent (*pulchritudo adhaerens*)." [13]

> The first presupposes no concept of what the object should be; the second does presuppose such a concept and, with it, an answering perfection of the object. Those of the first kind are said to be (self-subsisting) beauties of this or that thing; the other kind of beauty, being attached to a concept (conditioned beauty), is ascribed to Objects which come under the concept of a particular end.[14]

Under "free beauty" Kant listed the beauties of nature, abstract designs, and nonthematic music; but under "dependent beauty" Kant included any aesthetic object the judgment of which "presupposes a concept of the end that defines what the thing has to be, and consequently a concept of its perfection . . ." [15]

In considering neo-Aristotelianism's capacity for permitting or guiding re-creation, then, we confront the anomaly that the standards on which re-creation depends in the fine arts—standards requiring the attainment of certain norms in re-creation which distinguish it from a mere haphazard or gross response such as an art object might stimulate—these standards have no counterpart in neo-Aristotelian criticism.

It is tempting, but misleading, to attribute the difference between the aesthetic critic's relationship to fine arts and the neo-Aristotelian critic's relationship to the rhetorical discourse to the categorical opposition of fine art and rhetorical activity.

---

[13] Immanuel Kant, *Kant's Critique of Aesthetic Judgment*, James Creed Meredith, trans. (Oxford, England, 1911), p. 72.

[14] *Ibid.*

[15] *Ibid.*, p. 73.

Hoyt Hudson provided a distinction of this sort earlier in this century when he wrote, ". . . poetry is for the sake of expression; the impression on others is incidental. Rhetoric is for the sake of impression; the expression is secondary—an indispensable means." [16] Hudson's elaboration of this distinction makes it clear that he thought of poetry as an end in itself, containing its own values, while he held the values of rhetorical discourse to be external to it, owing to its instrumental character. If the rhetorical discourse works at all, in this view, it works to persuade its auditors. Their response alone can actually complete the process of which rhetorical discourse is a part. The audience's active participation in supplying enthymematic premises is an integral part of the Aristotelian conception of the persuasive process.[17]

This general view of the difference between poetry and rhetorical discourse implies the severe attenuation, if not the impossibility, of re-creation in neo-Aristotelianism because of the nature of rhetorical discourse itself. If there is re-creation at all, it is performed by the rhetor's immediate audience, not by the critic. The critic's task can only be to record this re-creation, if he can, as an integral part of the rhetorical transaction he appraises; but the critic's own response to the discourse is of no consequence, since the critical response is always distinct from the auditory response. Further, since this view minimizes or eliminates re-creation because of the nature of rhetorical discourse, then, it seems, it would minimize or eliminate it for *any* criticism of rhetorical discourse, not just for neo-Aristotelianism.

As we have observed, this is a tempting position because with it one can make an elegant argument; but it is misleading. It misleads by assuming a distinction between poetry and rhetorical

---

[16] Hoyt H. Hudson, "Rhetoric and Poetry," *Quarterly Journal of Speech Education*, 10 (April 1924), p. 146.

[17] A fuller discussion of this point is in Lloyd F. Bitzer, "Aristotle's Enthymeme Revisited," *Quarterly Journal of Speech*, XLV (December 1959), pp. 407–408. See also Edwin Black, "A Consideration of the Rhetorical Causes of Breakdown in Discussion," *Speech Monographs*, XXII (March 1955), p. 18.

discourse which does not, in fact, exist. Even Hudson, whose main concern was drawing a distinction between the two, no sooner made his distinction than he found it necessary to qualify it to the vanishing point. He was compelled to grant the existence of a "rhetorical element" in poetry, present in varying degrees,[18] and to grant the occurrence of poetic passages in rhetorical discourses.[19] Indeed, we have discourses that fall exactly between the "realms" of imaginative literature and rhetoric, as Hudson distinguished them, and these discourses solicit the attention of the critic as imperatively as any other. The Gettysburg Address is one such; Chapman's Coatesville Address, treated later in this chapter, is another. One may also think of *The Grapes of Wrath,* or *Crime and Punishment,* or *Gulliver's Travels,* or the *Annals* of Tacitus, or the *Symposium* of Plato, of the whole literature of social protest, of the genres of parody and satire, of countless sermons and epideictic discourses, even of such examples of "pure" poetry as *Paradise Lost* with its rhetorical objective of justifying "the ways of God to man."

The distinction will not do. There may be modest inquiries for which it may suffice, but it will not support an explanation for the inability of the neo-Aristotelian critic to perform recreation on the rhetorical discourse. We must find the explanation elsewhere—not in the nature of rhetorical discourse, but in the nature of neo-Aristotelian criticism.

Again we confront the characteristic preoccupation of the neo-Aristotelian critic with the rhetor's immediate audience and immediate situation, his tendency to accept the tactical objectives of the rhetor unquestioningly, as given, and to ask of the discourse only how well or ill it serves these objectives. It is the unique perspective imposed by such a critical position rather than rhetorical discourse itself that obviates re-creation.

The generic critic, responding re-creatively to the art object, attempts "to interpret it *correctly* as a vehicle of communica-

---

[18] Hudson, *op. cit.,* pp. 150–151.
[19] *Ibid.,* pp. 153–154.

tion." [20] In what does the correctness consist? "Really to re-
create . . . is to apprehend the content which its author actually
expressed in it . . .," to " 'feel' what we would judge . . .," to
have "an immediate artistic experience in the presence of the
work of art itself." In short, re-creation in generic criticism of
the fine arts involves the undistracted and unmediated confrontation of the critic with the work. Is such an enterprise
open to the neo-Aristotelian critic? Clearly, it is not. He approaches the work already convinced of the irrelevance of his
own responses. What difference does it make if, in studying the
Lincoln-Douglas debates, the neo-Aristotelian critic finds Douglas's repeatedly expressed indifference to the existence of slavery
a moral abomination? It is not, in neo-Aristotelianism, the critic's moral standards that will be exercised. Douglas's efforts will
be measured against the public morality of 1858; the standards
of Douglas's immediate audience will be interposed between
the critic and the discourse.

Rather than seek an interpretation of the discourse that real-
izes all that is in it and that aims "to see the object as it really
is," [21] the neo-Aristotelian critic attempts to make an estimate
of the historically factual effects of the discourse on its relatively immediate audience. The critic's own sensitivity may or
may not disclose anything, but even if it does whisper a soft
insinuation in his ear, that suggestion must be empirically con-
firmed in a way that aesthetic reactions cannot be—namely,
with reference to the audience rather than to the object of criticism. Indeed, the neo-Aristotelian critic's personal reaction even
to a contemporaneous discourse is of no importance unless the
reaction is shared by a large or significant segment of the speaker's audience. If the critic alone, of all the people in the United
States, responds favorably to the speech of a presidential aspir-
ant, his response is, because of its singularity, trivial to neo-
Aristotelian criticism. He can make no plea *for* the speech with-

---

[20] Greene, *op. cit.*, p. 371. My italics.
[21] T. S. Eliot, *The Sacred Wood* (London, 1948), p. 15.

out affecting the speech, without altering the object on which his criticism works.

In the very act of justifying the contemporaneous speech or its arguments, of revealing hitherto unremarked merits in the rhetorical discourse, the critic is contributing to the arguments themselves, so that a later assessment—a neo-Aristotelian assessment—of the historical significance of just that set of arguments must account for the critic's justifications and popularization of the speech in exactly the same way in which the speech itself is appraised. A literary critic, on the other hand, may argue *for* a poem so convincingly, illuminating its merits and the skill of its execution, that the poem comes to be accepted as fine literature and may even pass into the category of accepted touchstones of literature where the burden of critical proof passes to the poem's detractors. In generic criticism the poem would not be affected by the explication; if the criticism were sound, it would eventuate in its audience apprehending the poem "as it really is." The poem and its critique would always stand apart, and each would have to receive an independent appraisal that could not substantively affect a judgment of the other.

In the case of the rhetorical discourse from the past whose subject matter is no longer viable, the necessity for self-effacement weighs even more heavily on the neo-Aristotelian critic. No matter how much he may admire a discourse of the past on an obsolete subject, he dare not permit his admiration to color his criticism, for he is engaged in the appraisal of a historical force whose energies, insofar as he is concerned, have been spent, either by having been transformed into action, or by having been dissipated in a lost cause. Again let us be reminded that the neo-Aristotelian critic bears this relationship to the discourse of the past because of his point of view, because of his interest in rhetorical discourse as an arrangement of tactics adapted to the relatively immediate audience. Another critic, uninhibited by this conception, may have a more direct converse with the discourse. Another critic may find means other than his self-effacement to circumvent the discourse's ideological obsoleteness. But in the case of neo-Aristotelianism, the focus is on that set of effects which the discourse had on a particular audience, and that focus necessitates not re-creation, but historiography.

We must be careful to distinguish between critical re-creation and the reconstruction of a past event. The former is an act of perception and appreciation; it comprehends an object in the immediate present. The latter is historiography, and the present vitality of its subject is an irrelevance, perhaps even an impediment, to the historian. What is it to *re-create* a poem of Andrew Marvell? It is to read it attentively and without prejudice, to understand the lexical possibilities of every word, to comprehend all that is in the poem. Is a similar procedure open to the neo-Aristotelian critic of rhetorical discourse? Let us turn to one and see. The subject is an address delivered in the Senate by Henry Clay on February 5 and 6, 1850.

> On the morning of February 5 the "little, cramped up, and wholly insufficient corner of the Capitol known as the Senate chamber" was overflowing. . . . At 12 o'clock the main door of the Senate opened, and the ladies, presenting in their gay costumes all the colors of the long range of millinery stores of Division Street "pressed forward in a solid phalanx," filling every cranny of the chamber. The tense audience waited expectantly. . . .
>
> Clay had leaned heavily on the arm of a companion as he climbed the slippery steps to the Senate chamber that sparkling winter morning. "Old Hal" showed his age. His head, bald on top, was fringed with long gray hair, and his cheeks were sunken. But as usual his genial smile made its impression. He worked at his desk in the Senate chamber until Mangum moved to proceed to the order of the day. Quietly, he put his papers in his desk, and arose with consummate ease and grace. The applause was deafening. The excitement carried over to those who were unable to obtain admittance, and they renewed their efforts at all entrances. Wild shouts, "mingled jargon of oaths, imprecations, and explosions of laughter" interrupted the speaker, and it was some time before officials were able to restore order. . . .
>
> Clay opened the speech with a personal reference to impress his audience with the gravity of the crisis. "Mr. Presi-

dent, never, on any former occasion, have I risen under feelings of such deep solicitude. I have witnessed many periods of great anxiety, of peril, and of danger even to the country; but I have never before arisen to address any assembly so oppressed, so appalled, so anxious." He invoked God to still "the violence and rage of party" and prayed for aid in his efforts to this end. The source of existing tensions he ascribed to "the violence and intemperance of party spirit." Then to allay any personal suspicion that ambition plagued him, Clay assured the Senate that he would jostle no one "in the pursuit of these honors or that elevation" which any member might be seeking; but he still left the way open to preferment.[22]

Continuing his description of Clay's speech in the same manner, the critic concludes:

When the exhausted speaker finished his 2-day address, men and women rushed to congratulate him and shower on him evidence of deep personal affection. A reporter who heard the speech in its entirety commented: "Those who heard Mr. Clay's argument yesterday, and thought indifferently about it, were today irresistibly carried along by his peroration. . . . The orator was all animation, fire and impulse. . . ." Conservative and influential papers predicted that the plan [which Clay had advocated] would find no favor with extremists but that it would pave the way for the acceptance of some plan not degrading to different sections. Clay wrote to his son that "The speech has produced a powerful and salutary effect in the country and in Congress." The demand for printed copies of the speech was great. The *Daily Globe* announced that not less than 80,000 copies would be printed in Washington, and a notice of 2 weeks was required for all orders.[23]

This is the neo-Aristotelian critic's version of re-creation. It is his attempt to bring the discourse vividly before us. Obviously,

---

[22] Ernest J. Wrage, "Henry Clay" in *A History and Criticism of American Public Address*, vol. II, by William Norwood Brigance (ed.). Copyright 1943. McGraw-Hill Book Company. Used by permission. Also published by Russell and Russell, Inc., New York, 1960.

[23] *Ibid.*, pp. 629–630.

it is historical reconstruction, and equally obviously, it does not put us in possession of the discourse in the same way that Clay's contemporaries possessed it.

No matter how vividly the critic may make the past live in his pages, no matter with what incorruptible verisimilitude he may present it to us, it is still the past. The voices we hear speak from the grave. We do not have the power of choice with Clay's compromise on the Wilmot Proviso. *Our* assent is not being solicited; *our* convictions cannot be engaged. The doctrines embodied in Clay's speech are historical archaisms, and the modern audience cannot stand in the same relation to them as to the humblest aesthetic object.

It may be that the laws of thermodynamics have some metaphorical application to intellectual history; that the energy given an idea can never be completely destroyed; that the speech Henry Clay delivered in 1850 welded together a collocation of attitudes which, transmuted a thousand times, is still with us. It may be. But if it is, we do not know it, and we have no very conspicuous way of finding it out. When we read the speech of Henry Clay, we find it doctrinally archaic, and no critical mediation can restore its doctrinal vitality. Neither the most vivid reconstruction of the past nor the most strenuous efforts of our own imaginations can quite succeed in bringing us to occupy a mid-nineteenth century psyche.

The neo-Aristotelian critic's version of re-creation is an attempt to see the discourse in a specific context, but aesthetic re-creation is not a search for contexts; it is, if anything, anti-contextual. Its whole animus is the isolation of the work from all extraneous influences and ancillary considerations, so that the work may be comprehended in and for itself. Note Eliot's re-creative commentary on Marvell's *Coy Mistress*, and note too that this poem is more remote from us than Clay's speech by two hundred years:

The theme is one of the great traditional commonplaces of European literature. It is the theme of *O mistress mine*, of

Gather ye rosebuds, of *Go, lovely rose*; it is in the savage austerity of Lucretius and the intense levity of Catullus. Where the wit of Marvell renews the theme is in the variety and order of the images. In the first of the three paragraphs Marvell plays with a fancy which begins by pleasing and leads to astonishment.

> Had we but world enough and time,
> This coyness, lady, were no crime,
> . . . I would
> Love you ten years before the Flood,
> And you should, if you please, refuse
> Till the conversion of the Jews;
> My vegetable love should grow
> Vaster than empires and more slow. . . .

We notice the high speed, the succession of concentrated images, each magnifying the original fancy. When this process has been carried to the end and summed up, the poem turns suddenly with that surprise which has been one of the most important means of poetic effect since Homer:

> But at my back I always hear
> Time's winged chariot hurrying near,
> And yonder all before us lie
> Deserts of vast eternity. . . .

A modern poet, had he reached the height, would very likely have closed on this moral reflection. But the three strophes of Marvell's poem have something like a syllogistic relation to each other. After a close approach to the mood of Donne,

> then worms shall try
> that long-preserved virginity . . .
> The grave's a fine and private place,
> But none, I think, do there embrace,

the conclusion

> Let us roll all our strength and all
> Our sweetness up into one ball,
> And tear our pleasures with rough strife,
> Through the iron gates of life.

It will hardly be denied that this poem contains wit; but it may not be evident that this wit forms the crescendo and diminuendo of a scale of great imaginative power. The wit is not only combined with, but fused into, the imagination. We can easily recognize a witty fancy in the successive images . . . but this fancy is not indulged, as it sometimes is by Cowley or Cleveland, for its own sake. . . . In fact, this alliance of levity and seriousness (by which the seriousness is intensified) is a characteristic of the sort of wit we are trying to identify. . . . It is a quality of a sophisticated literature; a quality which expands in English just at the moment before the English mind altered . . . With our eye still on Marvell, we can say that wit is not erudition, as in much of Milton. It is not cynicism, though it has a kind of toughness which may be confused with cynicism by the tender-minded. It is confused with erudition because it belongs to an educated mind, rich in generations of experience; and it is confused with cynicism because it implies a constant inspection and criticism of experience. It involves, probably, a recognition, implicit in the expression of every experience, of other kinds of experience which are possible, which we find as clearly in the greatest as in poets like Marvell. Such a general statement may seem to take us a long way from *The Nymph and the Fawn*, or even from the *Horatian Ode*; but it is perhaps justified by the desire to account for that precise taste of Marvell's which finds for him the proper degree of seriousness for every subject which he treats. His errors of taste, when he trespasses, are not sins against this virtue; they are conceits, distended metaphors and similes, but they never consist in taking a subject too seriously or too lightly. This virtue of wit is not a peculiar quality of minor poets, or of the minor poets of one age or of one school; it is an intellectual quality which perhaps only becomes noticeable by itself, in the work of lesser poets. . . . The quality which Marvell had, this modest and certainly impersonal virtue—whether we call it wit or reason or even urbanity—we have patently failed to define. By whatever name we call it, and however we define that name, it is something precious and needed and apparently extinct; it is what should preserve the reputation of Marvell. . . .[24]

Here we find re-creative criticism shading off into and forming the foundation of judicial criticism. The quality of wit in the poem is disclosed, commented upon, and finally evaluated. The subject of the investigation is not Marvell's impact upon the seventeenth century. The only relevant responses to the poem are those of the critic. They are responses that can be shared by the critic's audience because both the critic and his audience are Marvell's audience as well.

We must note too what constitutes evidence for the assertions of re-creation as contrasted with reconstruction. Eliot's statements are supported by reference to the poem. There are, of course, references to other poems early in the quoted passage, and passing reference to other poems (Homer, Cleveland, Cowley), but these references are parts of the judicial thread that runs through the passage: the task of "estimating the value of a work of art in relation to other works of art"—to refer again to Greene's definition. The comments revealing the machinery of the poem always rely on the poem itself for confirmation. By contrast, Wrage's reconstruction must rely on other data than the speech for confirmation. The expectations of Clay's auditors, the reputation that Clay enjoyed, the testimony of those in attendance at the speech, all become indispensable data for the validation of Wrage's efforts. In sum, Eliot, the re-creative critic, focusses on the work itself; Wrage, the neo-Aristotelian critic, focusses on the interaction between the work and its immediate audience. Eliot regards the work in its timeless aspect; Wrage "regards a speech as a communication to a specific audi-

---

[24] From "Andrew Marvell" in *Selected Essays: New Edition by T. S. Eliot*, copyright 1932, 1936, 1950 by Harcourt, Brace & World, Inc., © 1960, by T. S. Eliot. Reprinted by permission of Harcourt, Brace & World, Inc., New York and Faber and Faber Ltd., London.

ence, and holds its [criticism's] business to be the analysis and appreciation of the orator's method of imparting his ideas to his hearers." [25]

As the selection from Wrage's critique illustrates, neo-Aristotelianism's closest approximation to re-creation is the effort to reconstruct the popular attitudes and prevailing sentiments of the time in history when the rhetorical discourse appeared.[26] This reconstruction involves the critic's thinking and feeling himself into the thoughts and feelings of the rhetor's immediate audience, so that he can empathize with that audience and attempt to gauge their reactions to the discourse. In this procedure, the critic's own reactions to the discourse play a decidedly subordinate role. He apprehends the discourse, insofar as he is able, via the minds of others. The success of the reconstruction turns on the suppression of the critic's own responses.

Now the question arises, What responses can a contemporary critic have to a rhetorical discourse of the past? How can the critic respond to, say, Clay's speech of 1850 when, as we have argued, that speech is doctrinally archaic? Is it even possible, for any critic, for any contemporary, to experience a reaction to a substantively dead discourse? Here we can only suggest an answer: the critic who believes that some techniques of argument can have an effect independent of the substance of argument is able to experience an immediate response to the discourse. If, in other words, a critic were to see any rhetorical discourse as working to make certain techniques conventional, to shape an audience's expectations for discourses that they will later hear or read, to mold an audience's sensibilities to language, then that critic would be in a position to respond with immediacy, even to a doctrinal archaism. He will be able to do so because, we shall assume, rhetorical techniques do not become

---

[25] Herbert A. Wichelns, "The Literary Criticism of Oratory," *The Rhetorical Idiom. Essays in Rhetoric, Oratory, Language, and Drama*, ed. Donald C. Bryant (Ithaca, N.Y., 1958), p. 5.

[26] For further examples of this historical reconstruction see Herbert L. Curry, "John C. Calhoun," Brigance, *A History and Criticism of American Public Address*, II, pp. 639–664; Hochmuth, *American Speeches*, pp. 21–71.

archaic in the way that doctrines and issues become archaic; a rhetorical technique will almost always stand as a live possibility at any point in history. We must defer the explication of this position until we can see it illustrated in specific discourses, to be treated subsequently. It may suffice for now merely to indicate its possibility and, thereby, to see neo-Aristotelianism in bolder relief.

The neo-Aristotelian critic is preoccupied with the immediate audience of the discourse; in a sense, his eye is where that audience's eyes are: on the issues of the discourse, on its doctrines, on the ideas to which the audience is asked to assent. And insofar as his focus is thus, then his own responses to the discourse will have no place in the critical performance. In the case of the doctrinally archaic discourse, he cannot even have any responses except as he is able to dissolve himself into the past. Such historical reconstruction may be enlightening, but its limits are severe. What Wellek and Warren say of the literary critic is no less true of the critic of rhetorical discourse.

> It is simply not possible to stop being men of the twentieth century while we engage in a judgment of the past; we cannot forget the associations of our own language, the newly acquired attitudes, the impact and the import of the last centuries. We cannot become contemporary readers of Homer or Chaucer or members of the audience of the theater of Dionysus in Athens or of the Globe in London. There will always be a decisive difference between an act of imaginative reconstruction and actual participation in a past point of view. We cannot really believe in Dionysus and laugh at him at the same time, as the audience of Euripides' *Bacchae* seems to have done; and few of us can accept Dante's circles of Hell and mountain of Purgatory as literal truth. If we should really be able to reconstruct the meaning which *Hamlet* held for its contemporary audience, we would merely impoverish it. We would suppress legitimate meanings which later generations found in *Hamlet*. We would bar the possibility of a new interpretation.[27]

---

[27] Rene Wellek and Austin Warren, *Theory of Literature* (New York, 1956), p. 31.

How much more unlikely it is that the rhetorical critic can make himself really concerned over Macedonia's designs on the Hellenic city-states, or the question of the slave trade in Africa, or even whether Calvin Coolidge should be elected President.

Clearly, neo-Aristotelianism leaves no provision for re-creation as that function is understood in generic criticism. This conclusion is, simply, a matter of fact. Whether it is a reassuring or a lamentable fact, whether it bodes well or ill for neo-Aristotelian criticism, or if it does not affect its efficacy at all, remains to be determined. It is equally clear that this fact must be appraised if we are to arrive at a view of the potentialities of neo-Aristotelianism as a critical system. It will be better assessed in conjunction with other conclusions to be drawn from a consideration of neo-Aristotelianism and the judicial aspect of criticism.

Before we leave, even temporarily, our consideration of re-creation in neo-Aristotelianism, we must note one position that has received some attention in literary circles. This is an argument, developed by some literary critics, that the themes and doctrines embodied in poetry, either because these doctrines enjoy a sort of argumentative neutrality or because they are so abstract as to be unaffected by time, have an imperviousness to obsolescence that is not shared by works of controversy, specifically, by rhetorical discourse.[28] These critics hold that great poems have an enduring vitality, regardless of their ideological content, which is denied works of rhetoric. The subject matter of rhetorical discourse is held to be of limited and transient interest, and the issues of polemic resolve themselves or grow old and die, the passionate immediacies of one generation becoming the quaint antiquities of the next. The implication of this view for re-creative criticism is that while the literary critic can and must depend on his own personal reaction to a literary

---

[28] For elaborations of this argument see I. A. Richards, *Principles of Literary Criticism* (New York, 1928), chs. 32–35; and *Practical Criticism* (London, 1930), ch. VIII; David Daiches, *A Study of Literature for Readers and Critics* (Ithaca, N.Y., 1948), pp. 61ff.

work of any age, the rhetorical critic, unless he deals with a contemporaneous rhetorical object, can have no comparable experience with the discourse. The rhetorical discourse becomes obsolete in a way to which the poem is immune.

This view of the relative importance of ideology to poetry and rhetoric, respectively, is far from satisfying. One cannot imagine how those critics who defend the view could offer definitive evidence of its truth, just as it is difficult to imagine how the view could be refuted with finality. The problem of what would constitute evidence seems insoluble. More likely, the question of whether the aesthetic critic insists on the primacy of content in poetry or whether he waives it as an aesthetically irrelevant accoutrement will depend on his critical objective of the moment. What is noteworthy is that some literary critics can, under some circumstances, ignore the literal content of poetry, can ignore Dante's "circles of Hell and mountain of Purgatory," to discern the attitudes, the assumptions, the moral economy that lie below the level of ideology. We do not find neo-Aristotelian critics doing this because, for them, the rhetorical discourse is nothing when abstracted from its doctrines.

We have already argued that the neo-Aristotelian's inability to re-create the discourse of the past stems from his preoccupation with the immediate audience rather than from the nature of rhetorical discourse. We would reiterate here that, arguments to the contrary notwithstanding, we have too many examples of rhetorical discourses that retain their doctrinal vitality and too many examples of poems that have lost theirs (but yet remain great poems) to subscribe to any firm distinctions between poetry and rhetoric. The argument cited above, defended at times by Richards and by Daiches, is serviceable only in reminding us that the neo-Aristotelian critic's focus on the immediate issues of a discourse does not necessarily exhaust the discourse. As the practice of literary criticism has occasionally suggested, there are other foci available. The fact that the neo-Aristotelian critics of rhetorical discourse do not avail themselves of these options, but instead focus steadily on the doctrines that do perish may be put down as a defining characteristic of neo-Aristotelianism, a characteristic that, perhaps more than any other, makes it incapable of re-creation.

JUDICIAL CRITICISM

The application of judicial criticism by neo-Aristotelian critics would seem, on casual consideration, to be a relatively uncomplicated matter. Passing evaluative judgment is so common an occurrence that hardly anyone hesitates to do so confidently. Rhetorical discourses especially are susceptible to many sorts of assessments, some not disinterested or insightful, but some—such as ethical assessments, logical assessments, and aesthetic assessments—perfectly legitimate and interesting. However, our special concern at present with neo-Aristotelian criticism raises more particular questions: whether there is any sort of judgment that can be uniquely well rendered by it, from its canons, or that is its special province in its judicial aspect; or, on the other hand, whether the adjudicatory function of neo-Aristotelian criticism is entirely that of collecting judgments founded on nonrhetorical values.

These questions are suggested by the fact that, while there are some kinds of judgments common to judicial criticism in all fields—for example, judgments of social utility and moral quality, other kinds of judgments are particular to certain kinds of objects—for example, judgments of harmonics, thematic development, and orchestration in music; color, balance, and texture in painting; imagery, characterization, and point of view in literature. The list could be extended and refined indefinitely to include not only judgments particular to other arts, like the dance, architecture, sculpture, dramatic staging, and others, but even to include judgments appropriate only to particular genres of art, like accessibility of exits in the design of airline terminals, or placement of *luftpausen* in song composition. Is there, then, any kind of judgment that would be involved in the judicial aspect of neo-Aristotelian criticism, especially important to it, or requisite to its successful execution?

These questions have received surprisingly few answers in the modern history of rhetorical criticism. Discussion of the subject of judicial criticism in neo-Aristotelianism has tended to resolve itself into a bifurcation, with only two opposing points of view actively soliciting the allegiance of critics. One view was expressed in an essay to which we have already alluded.

> If now we turn to rhetorical criticism . . . we find that its point of view is patently single. It is not concerned with permanence, nor yet with beauty. It is concerned with effect. It regards a speech as a communication to a specific audience, and holds its business to be the analysis and appreciation of the orator's method of imparting his ideas to his hearers.[29]

As Redding has pointed out, the uniqueness of the critical position enunciated by Wichelns lay in its endorsement of "effect" as the prime criterion of rhetorical criticism; not in the methods of criticism that Wichelns countenanced.[30] In methodology, Wichelns submitted the Aristotelian categories.[31]

The alternate view, more recently affirmed, was expressed by Parrish.

> . . . the critic should not be diverted into an attempt to assess the *result* of a speech except as its effect may help us to judge the quality of the speech itself. Rhetoric, strictly speaking, is not concerned with the *effect* of a speech, but with its *quality*, and its quality can be determined quite apart from its effect.[32]

As we shall see, Parrish too is neo-Aristotelian in his critical methodology.

At issue is the question of what constitutes the aim of judicial

---

[29] Wichelns, *op. cit.*, p. 35.

[30] Charles Redding, "Extrinsic and Intrinsic Criticism," *Western Speech*, XXI (Spring 1957), p. 98.

[31] Wichelns, *op. cit.*, pp. 32–39.

[32] Wayland Maxfield Parrish, "The Study of Speeches," Parrish and Hochmuth, *American Speeches* (New York, 1954), p. 7. Parrish's italics.

criticism in rhetoric, and the issue is joined in these two quotations. Wichelns's view, in its insistence that the essence of the rhetorical judgment is the assessment of an interaction between rhetor and audience, can be characterized as the pragmatic position, since it holds that the consequences of a rhetorical discourse are the key material for evaluation. The position urged in the Parrish paper will hereafter be called formalistic criticism because it would render a judgment of the discourse as a self-contained unit, without regard for any particular audience. Each view must be examined in more detail, not only to discover the extent of actual disagreement between them, but also, inasmuch as the two views represent a schism within neo-Aristotelianism, to determine if either view suggests a strictly rhetorical judgment appropriate to the judicial aspect of neo-Aristotelian criticism.

Parrish's own elaboration and defense of formalistic criticism, because his position is more familiar to generic critical theory, invites investigation, after which other elaborations of the view will be considered. The central question arising from Parrish's defense of formalism is, What is "quality"? Inasmuch as the quality of a speech is to be assessed, any possible clarification of quality should help illuminate the critical position of formalism.

In his essay, Parrish discusses rhetorical categories gleaned from the works of Aristotle, especially as modified by Cicero, as the proper topics of judicial criticism. These topics are listed as character (*ethos*), content (*inventio*), logic (*logos*), arrangement (*dispositio*), motivation (*pathos*), and style (*elocutio*).[33] Parrish acknowledges his debt to Aristotle's *Rhetoric* in the formulation of these standards.[34] While systematic definition is absent from the Parrish essay, these standards or topics seem to be intended to stand as constituents of quality. Taking them in this way, let us see if quality can be considered a rhetorical value, one that, as Parrish claims, is different from and more important than effect.

---

[33] Parrish, *op. cit.*, pp. 13–19.
[34] *Ibid.*, p. 12.

The Parrish paper offers two justifications of quality as the paramount value of rhetorical judgment: tradition and "persuasiveness." The first of these does not, of course, precisely constitute a justification. While it is eminently true that the endorsement of an idea by a genius of Aristotle's stature is certainly a *prima facie* reason for giving that idea careful and serious consideration, still such an endorsement does not reinforce or justify the idea in any logical sense. Therefore, we might not be unfair in taking the citation of authority and tradition in the Parrish paper as immaterial to the argument.

The second and more interesting justification of the value of quality in the paper is what is referred to as "persuasiveness." [35] Parrish refers to the topics of criticism as ". . . some of the most important means by which a speech works persuasion in those who hear and judge it." [36] Ethos is referred to as ". . . one of the most important elements in persuasiveness . . ." [37] Content is called ". . . the second element of effectiveness . . ." [38] Emotional appeal is ". . . another means of persuasion, and perhaps the most important of all . . ." [39] Style is ". . . another important means of persuasion . . ." [40]

Surely the persistent reiteration of the constituents of quality as "means of persuasion" is no accident. We must take it as indicating the sort of formalistic judgment that Parrish advocates. When Parrish writes that rhetoric is concerned with assessing the quality of a discourse, he evidently means that rhetoric is concerned with assessing the means of persuasion in a discourse. The idea is the Aristotelian view of rhetoric as the faculty of discovering in any given case the available means of persuasion. [41]

---

[35] *Ibid.*, pp. 13–19 et passim.
[36] *Ibid.*, p. 13.
[37] *Ibid.*
[38] *Ibid.*
[39] *Ibid.*, p. 15.
[40] *Ibid.*, p. 17.
[41] Aristotle, *Rhetoric*, 1355b, 11. 26–27.

The next question that would arise in the Parrish position would be, By what means is quality to be appraised? Parrish's only suggestion of an answer lies in his use of the term persuasive, and we can go no further in this examination without raising the question, What is meant by *persuasive?* We are able to discern in general usage of the term persuasive at least four distinct meanings. One way we seem to use the word is to describe what we take to be the intent of a discourse —for example, "He was trying to be persuasive instead of merely giving advice," or "He wrote a persuasive editorial instead of an impartial report."

A second use of *persuasive* is to describe the consequences of a discourse—for example, "Such and such a speech was quite persuasive before that audience," meaning that the audience accepted the ideas of the speech or, in some way, behaved as the speaker wanted. This second usage of the term entails what the Wichelns essay holds to be the distinctive judgment of rhetorical criticism.

The third general usage of *persuasive* is as a psychological report of personal reaction to a speech. The way in which *persuasive* is used in this sense is to express approval of a discourse and to indicate that one has oneself been influenced by it; for example, if, after hearing a speech, an auditor says, "That was a very persuasive speech," we may well interpret him as reporting approbation of the ideas expressed and also as reporting the psychological fact that he has been moved or influenced by those ideas.

Finally, there is a use of *persuasive* suggested by the Parrish paper—the evaluative use. What is meant by *persuasive* in this sense? Parrish's position is that a persuasive speech is one that meets the conditions of persuasion enumerated in his paper as critical standards or topics. The critical topics constitute the quality of a speech. Since it is the quality of the speech that is to be evaluated, and this quality is to be evaluated by its persuasiveness, and the constituents of persuasiveness are the topics again, the argument of the Parrish paper is that quality must be evaluated by quality. The argument, then, is invalidated by its circularity, and we must look elsewhere for a suitable defense of the formalistic position in neo-Aristotelian criticism.

Inasmuch as all the usages of *persuasive* suggested above were exemplified except the evaluative usage alleged by Parrish, perhaps some defense of the formalistic position can be found in a sense of *persuasive* that clearly does not fit any of the categories except the evaluative. Such an example may be "He spoke very persuasively, but he did not win the case." This does seem to be an evaluative use of the term persuasive in that it seems to refer to some quality of the speech while specifically detaching the judgment from a consideration of effect.

When we consider the example more carefully, we can see that it is not, after all, a clear case of the formalistic judgment. The example can be translated in only one way that does not do violence to its apparent meaning, but yet does not employ *persuasive* in a nonevaluative sense: "He did not win *not* because of his own failure in speaking, but for some other reason." The first question that would occur to one upon hearing some statement such as that contained in the example would be, Why, then, did he lose? The fact that this question is raised by the example further suggests the accuracy of the proposed translation. And what is the translation but a statement about effect? The statement seems not so much to attribute any quality to the speech, or to make a positive assessment of the speech, as to deny that the speech produced the effects that occurred. Whatever the critical value of such a statement, it is not a formalistic judgment, at least not in the sense in which, as it was defined earlier, the formalistic judgment is one divorced from a consideration of effects. It is, rather, a pragmatic judgment, and this was not the object of our present inquiry.

In seeking to discover if the neo-Aristotelian position will yield a formalistic judgment, as Parrish seems to believe, it may be well to waive Parrish's own development of his views, and to test a more promising argument that Parrish, or some other formalist, may advance. The formalist may hold that though he is able to use *good* in a rhetorical sense, that is, to call a discourse rhetorically good without referring to its ethical, aesthetic, or logical quality or to its effects, what passes for critical topics in the Parrish paper serves only to clarify this use of *good*, but not to define it with finality. The formalist may say further, "If asked to evaluate a speech, I may say of it that though it was effective, it was not rhetorically good. Unless this assessment can be proved meaningless, it is obvious that I would be passing a formalistic judgment, inasmuch as I would have explicitly divorced the effects of the speech from any appraisal of it."

In order to understand more clearly what the formalist is saying, we may ask him why he denied that the speech was rhetorically good. He can give either of two replies: (1) he may say that the audience was already strongly inclined to believe the speaker's proposal and that this predisposition accounted for the effects, that all the audience needed was someone to make the proposal, that just about any speech that advanced the desired proposal would have been effective, and that, as a matter of fact, the speech in question was boring and had incoherent passages in it; (2) he may say that while the audience acclaimed the speech and was brought to hold certain convictions because of it, the organization, style, and use of evidence of the speech could have been improved and were, therefore, deficient when measured against an ideal standard.

In the event that the first reason was advanced, it would not be at all clear that the formalist was accurate in calling the speech effective, or that he really maintained any distinction between *effective* and *good*. We should probably consider it a strange sort of response to describe a speech, or anything else, as *effective* while holding that the thing so described contributed negligibly or not at all to the results produced. It seems that part of what we mean by *effective* is "contributing substantially to the production of effects."

The second reason seems to be the stronger of the two. The formalist can defend his position by saying, "The fact that I am not able to provide an exhaustive definition of *rhetorically good* does not mean that I cannot use the term meaningfully. I am able to tell you when a speech is not good, and the reasons for its not being good, and I can infer some of the characteristics of this good by converting these reasons to different forms. I can justify my appraisals of specific discourses by recourse to generally accepted touchstones of rhetorical excellence—Demosthenes, Cicero, Edmund Burke, for example—and show the relative merit of a discourse by comparing it to these touchstones. Thus, I would in a sense be defining *rhetorically good* by example. This may not be a generic definition, but it is a common procedure in ethics and in aesthetics, and I can apply it equally well to rhetorical discourses. In short, I can apply the term rhetorically good to specific cases and demonstrate that it is divorced from the effects of the discourse being assessed."

So long as the formalist held to this position and remained consistent with it in his criticism, he would seem to be on very firm ground indeed. We must, of course, be careful to understand what the "touchstone" system of criticism implies and what it does not imply. Obviously, no critic could reasonably demand of a contemporary rhetor that he speak in exactly the same way as, say, Edmund Burke. Touchstones are not models for copying. Rather, the touchstone system would demand that the contemporary rhetor treat his subject as well as Burke treated his before the contemporary would be awarded the highest accolade. This does not mean that the contemporary must organize his materials in the same way as Burke, employ evidence from the same sources as Burke, share the philosophical assumptions of Burke, or duplicate the vocabulary of Burke.

What the touchstone system seems to imply is that the critic, or anyone else who cares to, can, by acquainting himself with the discourses of Burke, come to hold certain expectations of what rhetorical discourse ought to do, and he can achieve certain insights into what rhetorical discourse is capable of doing. These expectations and insights do not provide him with explicit, mechanically applicable standards; they provide him with that vague quality, *taste*, without which no set of explicit standards can be judiciously applied. The touchstone system, then, is extremely useful to the training of the critic, to the sharpening of his perceptions and the elevation of his expectations. And he, in turn, puts the touchstone to a similar use when, in comparing to it the discourse that is being appraised, he trains the auditors of his criticism to make high demands of rhetorical discourse. More to the point, the formalist is in a strong position so long as he employs touchstones to define, by example, *rhetorically good.*

It is only when the judgment of rhetorical criticism is sanctioned by fixed principles rather than by recourse to touchstones that formalism is undermined—undermined in the sense that what passes for a formalistic judgment is usually a pragmatic judgment at bottom. This claim can best be clarified through a specific illustration. One standard, for example, that neo-Aristotelian critics have invoked in appraising discourses is that of "good organization." One critic has suggested "clear, logical development" as a criterion for the assessment of sermons.[42] Another notes, of Jonathan Edwards, "Clear organization is one of the outstanding characteristics of Edwards' speaking." [43] Have we, in this standard of good organization, a principle applicable to discourses without regard for their effects on audiences? If we have, then the formalistic position as it is defended by Parrish can be said to be established. Moreover, the judicial application of other principles, derived from Aristotle's *Rhetoric* —the analysis of ethos, for example—would receive strong encouragement. In order to find out if we have so viable a standard, we must inquire into why a discourse ought to be well organized and what rhetorical theorists of the past have said on the subject of organization.

Plato, in his writings on rhetoric, avoids specific prescriptions

---

[42] George V. Bohman, "The Colonial Period," Brigance, A *History and Criticism of American Public Address,* I, p. 23.

[43] Orville Hitchcock, "Jonathan Edwards," Brigance, *op. cit.,* I, p. 222. Similar uses of "good organization" as a standard for judgment are to be found throughout the three volumes of this work.

and detailed analysis of rhetorical conventions. His concern is to place rhetoric with propriety into the general encyclopedia of learning, and to assess its social and ethical functions.[44] However, he does provide a theoretical foundation for organization as a critical concept. There are two parts to this concept: arrangement is to be determined by dialectical necessity [45] and by the demands of the audience.[46]

Plato seemed to conceive of a natural order appropriate to, if not inhering in, discourse: ". . . every discourse ought to be a living creature, having a body of its own and a head and feet; there should be a middle, beginning, and end, adapted to one another and to the whole." [47]

Later, speaking of the true or ideal rhetor, Socrates says, ". . . having classified men and speeches, and their kinds and affections, and adapted them to one another, he will tell the reasons of his arrangement, and show why one soul is persuaded by a particular form of argument and another not." [48]

Plato proposes two principles of composition related to arrangement:

First, the comprehension of scattered particulars in one idea; as in our definition of love, which whether true or false certainly gave clearness and consistency to the discourse, the speaker should define his several notions and so make his meaning clear. . . . The second principle is that of division into species according to the natural formation, where the joint is, not breaking any part as a bad carver might.[49]

One of Plato's two principles of arrangement seems to be pragmatic and the other to be formal. The concept of arrange-

---

[44] See Edwin Black, "Plato's View of Rhetoric," *Quarterly Journal of Speech*, XLIV (December 1958), pp. 361–374.

[45] Plato, *Phaedrus*, sec. 264.

[46] *Ibid.*, sec. 277.

[47] Plato, *Phaedrus*, sec. 264, Benjamin Jowett, trans. (New York, 1892).

[48] *Ibid.*, sec. 271.

[49] *Ibid.*, sec. 266.

ment being born of clarity is pragmatic in that the effect of the arrangement on the auditor's comprehension of the discourse is the determinant of the arrangement itself; and the concept of there being a natural formation inhering in discourse is clearly formalistic, or at least, a formalistic manner of expression. But it is the analytic aspect of dialectic that is referred to in the concept of "natural formation." [50] Plato was clear on the persuasiveness of this dialectical analysis. His doctrines included a belief in the presence of knowledge in men from their births, a doctrine most dramatically presented in the interrogation of the slave in *Meno*. This belief explains the persuasiveness of the formalistic principle, and in so doing converts the principle from formalistic to pragmatic. The natural division of a subject is that division that is perceived as natural by all men since it corresponds to the inherent arrangement of their minds. Hence, what at first appeared to be a formalistic justification of good organization turns out, on closer examination, to have rhetorical utility because of its adaptation to men, that is, its effects. Plato, then, provides us with no formalistic principle of arrangement.

In Aristotle's discussion of arrangement we find, first, a repudiation of the plethora of organizational principles that earlier rhetoricians recommended.[51] Statement and Argument are the only two sections of the speech that Aristotle regards as necessary, a necessity he infers from a definition of what constitutes a speech rather than from an investigation of the forms of speeches actually delivered.[52] Statement and Argument are the "essential features," [53] to which may be added Proem and Epilogue to exhaust the possibilities.

Clearly, Aristotle conceives of Proem and Epilogue as functioning to create in the audience a state of mind or disposition

---

[50] See Francis Macdonald Cornford, *Plato's Theory of Knowledge* (London, 1935), pp. 263–264.

[51] Aristotle, *Rhetoric*, bk. 3, ch. 13.

[52] *Ibid.*

[53] *Ibid.*, W. Rhys Roberts, trans. (New York, 1954).

favorable to the speaker by allaying their prejudices, transmitting a flattering impression of the speaker, or assisting the audience's memory. These functions are grudgingly conceded: "They are for the audience, an audience that is weak enough to accept utterances beside the point . . ." [54] Yet, grudging or not, the grounds for this concession are revelatory of Aristotle's conception of arrangement, for obviously the parts of the speech are conceived by him functionally rather than organically, and they are to be judged by their effects on the audience.

The pragmatic tendency we find in Aristotle's treatment of arrangement we also find in the less original treatments of Cicero and Quintilian. As Wagner put it, after reviewing the leading theories of arrangement in the ancient rhetorics, ". . . in the greatest of the ancient rhetorics—by implication in Aristotle's, and by explicit and repeated statement of scope and nature in the others—*dispositio* was conceived as planned adaptation." [55] Thonssen and Baird summarize the view of ancient rhetoricians even more fully:

> The parts of a speech were conceived in terms of function, of operational utility. Consequently, their names are unimportant, so long as the tasks assigned to the units are adequately fulfilled. Because simplicity is a virtue in this instance, many rhetorical critics use the Aristotelian plan of organization as the criterion for evaluating *disposition*. This would seem to be a defensible standard since the critic is not interested in form for its own sake, but rather for the contribution it makes in eliciting a desired response from hearers.[56]

In sum, those ancients who laid down the theoretical foundations of neo-Aristotelian criticism functioned pragmatically in

---

[54] Aristotle, *Rhetoric*, 1414b, Lane Cooper, trans. (New York, 1932).

[55] Russell H. Wagner, "The Meaning of Dispositio," *Studies in Speech and Drama in Honor of Alexander M. Drummond*, ed. Herbert A. Wichelns (Ithaca, N.Y., 1944), p. 291.

[56] Lester Thonssen and A. Craig Baird, *Speech Criticism. The Development of Standards for Rhetorical Appraisal* (New York, 1948), p. 398.

developing their critical standards. Where we find *dispositio* treated in critical writing as if it were an organic quality of discourse to be divorced from the general effects of language, we have encountered a corruption of the ancient analysis. Even if we approach the principle of good organization analytically rather than historically in an effort to determine what constitutes the good organization of prose compositions, we still find that the effect of the discourse is the ultimate standard, even of its organization.

One possible explanation of good organization is that the good pattern represents the pattern of intellectual activity by which an individual comes to hold a conviction. Thus, the acceptable pattern is a projection of the process of intellection by which beliefs are acquired. Plato, at one point, can be interpreted as hinting at such a view.[57] This view is pragmatic since it bases its critical value respecting organization on the demand that the ordering of a discourse conform to the intellectual requirements of the audience.

A second possible explanation is that the good pattern of organization presents the series of conditions through which an audience must be brought in order to be persuaded. Aristotle suggests such a view in advising the pacification of the audience as an early stage in the persuasive speech.[58] This is again a pragmatic value since it is based on audience effects.

A third possible explanation is that the good pattern of organization is a process whereby symbols are enriched in connotation by their appearing in a certain relationship to one another. Poetic and dramatic works are often assessed in this way. For example, in Ibsen's *Ghosts*, the pathos and dramatic impact of Oswald's calling for the sun in the last scene turns on the whole play that preceded. If Oswald called for the sun in the first act, his gesture would be impoverished. An example closer to rhetorical discourse is Mark Antony's speech to the

---

[57] Plato, *Phaedrus*, 277c.
[58] Aristotle, *Rhetoric*, 1414b.

Roman mob in Shakespeare's *Julius Caesar*. The recurrent phrase "honorable men" gains in ironically accusatory force as the speech progresses because of its accumulation of pejorative connotation.[59] Rearrange the speech, and the phrase would lose its force toward the end of the passage in which it recurs. This view of organization, too, is pragmatic in that it explains the dispositional value of criticism in terms, ultimately, of audience effects.

Of course, these explanations do not contradict one another, nor does any one of them demand exclusivity. They may all be operative in a given case where organization is good, or one may apply to one case and another to another. The point is that they are all pragmatic in their sanctions.

What is true of organization as a rhetorical value is probably also true of other principles of judgment that may be subsumed under neo-Aristotelianism; these standards are sanctioned by the fact that they produced certain desired effects in audiences. To confirm the generalization we have only to consider how any standard can be justified. The justification, as Thonssen and Baird have noted, must always come back to "eliciting a desired response from the hearers," which is to say, *effect*. When the neo-Aristotelian critic appraises the quality of a discourse in terms of criteria derived from the Aristotelian tradition, the ultimate justification of these criteria is effect. Only when the critic justifies some particular judgment of his with recourse to a touchstone is he delivering a purely formalistic judgment.

There is a point beyond which the distinction between the formalistic and the pragmatic judgments is a quibble. That point is defined by the critic's very conception of *effect*. When the effects of a discourse are understood by the critic to be only those that a discourse has on the beliefs of its immediate audience, then the distinction between the formalistic judgment and the pragmatic judgment is a substantial one. It is substantial because the pragmatic judgment limits the critic's view to the

---

59 Cf. Kenneth Burke, "Antony in Behalf of the Play," *The Philosophy of Literary Form* (New York, 1957), pp. 279–290.

circumscribed transaction between a rhetor and an audience isolated in time, while the formalistic judgment tends to ignore the specific audience entirely, having invoked what is assumed to be timeless standards. When, however, the conception of *effect* comprehends more than the immediate audience, the judgment rendered comes increasingly to resemble the judgment of formalism.

A critic can, after all, interest himself not alone in the short-range effect of a discourse on its immediate audience, but also in its effect on later audiences and its indirect effects to the extent that all of these audiences, under the influence of the discourse, themselves exert influence in speaking, writing, and acting. He can inquire into the effects of the arguments, the message of the discourse, and the effects of its ways of arguing—its rhetorical techniques, which may have consequences quite distinct from its arguments. He can legitimately investigate the effects of the discourse on the rhetor, on what it does to his public image and his personal convictions. He can appraise its effects on subsequent discourses of the same rhetor, on those of other rhetors on the same subject, on those of other rhetors on other subjects, and its effects on the memory and influence of previous rhetors and discourses as they are reappraised by audiences and by the critic himself in the light of a new rhetorical event. The critic can, in short, assess all the differences a rhetorical discourse has made in the world and will make, and how the differences are made and why. This range of interests will take the critic far beyond the simple mechanics of polling an audience, or measuring the volume of their applause. And insofar as these effects are consequences of a wide range of human experience, there can be no separating them from any abstract "quality" that solicits our humane interest. Understanding *effect* so broadly would dissipate the formalist-pragmatic dichotomy and tend to resolve the differences between the positions of Parrish and Wichelns. However, *effect* is not this comprehensively understood in the practice of neo-Aristotelian criticism.

As our consideration of the historical aspect of neo-Aristotelian criticism has argued, the neo-Aristotelian critic is usually concerned with the immediate audience and the immediate situation. His tendency is to appraise the discourse in terms of its efficacy in fulfilling the ideological objectives of the rhetor. If the discourse has other effects, unrelated to these ideological objectives, the neo-Aristotelian critic does not take them into account. Or, if the discourse has none but immediate, ideological effects, the neo-Aristotelian critic does not account for its transience as an influence. Neo-Aristotelianism, then, is pragmatic in its judicial aspect, and pragmatic in a limited sense of that term.

SUMMARY

We are now in a position to draw some general conclusions about the adequacy of neo-Aristotelian criticism to discharge the general functions of criticism. Taking for our frame of reference Greene's tripartite division of generic criticism, we can see that neo-Aristotelianism demands a full exercise of historical criticism, although it circumscribes the conception of context that will guide this criticism; [60] it substitutes historical reconstruction for re-creative criticism; and it limits judicial criticism to the evaluation of immediate effects. These three characteristics of neo-Aristotelianism are intimately related.

---

[60] A special group of literary critics, mainly specialists in sixteenth- and seventeenth-century English literature, are sometimes called rhetorical critics. The interests of these critics and the nature of their investigations rather clearly place them in Greene's category of historical criticism, since they tend to explicate poetry and drama by determining the ideological and educational influences on authors. See, e.g., Rosamund Tuve, *Elizabethan and Metaphysical Imagery; Renaissance Poetic and Twentieth-Century Critics* (Chicago, 1947); and Ruth Wallerstein, *Studies in Seventeenth-Century Poetic* (Madison, Wis., 1950), esp. ch. 2, "Schooling and Approaches to Theory," on pp. 11–58. They are called rhetorical critics because they trace the formal doctrine of literary composition that guided poets of the sixteenth and seventeenth centuries to rhetorics of those and earlier centuries. Since the rubric rhetorical criticism refers only to this sort of historical investigation when applied to works of these scholars, I shall take no account of them here.

Re-creative criticism can occur only as the object being criticized has effects on the critic. The neo-Aristotelian criticism of rhetorical discourse does not allow for an effect of the discourse on the critic because its conception of the discourse's context does not include the critic. In practice, this theoretical position has the considerable advantage of minimizing the writing of impressionistic criticism in rhetoric. Since neo-Aristotelianism allows no place for the personal revelations of the critic, the neo-Aristotelian critic is less likely than he would otherwise be to compose effusions or embarrassing confessionals in his exegesis of a rhetorical discourse.

It is the sort of invidious comparison that is dangerous to make and impossible finally to prove, but a casual inventory of rhetorical critiques compared with a random collection of literary critiques probably would reveal a somewhat crisper objectivity in the former, a lesser tendency to lay bare the soul. One would likely find the person of the literary critic obtruding more into his criticism, and almost invariably this personal obtrusion would hinder an understanding of the literary work. Sometimes—though rarely—the critic himself is a man of such unusual gifts that his self-portraiture becomes an artful work, and his criticism can be read for its own sake. Sometimes, too, the critic is a man of such acute sensitivity that his personal revelations in converse with a work of art do shed light on the potentialities of the work. One can readily admit that what a play or a piece of music did to George Bernard Shaw, for example, can still reveal as much about the work of art as about Shaw, because Shaw's reactions were exceedingly well informed and well disciplined. But the fact remains that criticism as a revelation of the work being criticized is more valuable than criticism as a record of the critic's inner life. Except in the hands of a very, very few men, the critical methodology that minimizes the personal responses, peculiar tastes, and singularities of the critic will be superior to the one that does not. In this regard, neo-Aristotelian criticism has undeniable value. By excluding the critic from the context of the discourse, by disallowing re-creation, and by sanctioning only the sort of judgment that can be empirically verified, neo-Aristotelianism has provided a methodology that, independently applied by different men to the same object, can yield the same conclusions. Neo-Aristotelianism has the advantage of objectivity.

However, neo-Aristotelianism has a concomitant defect, and that defect is equivocation. The same characteristics of his methodology that make for the neo-Aristotelian critic's objectivity also place him in a deferential posture. It is the rhetor to whom he defers—the rhetor whose discourse he is appraising.

Let us be reminded once again of the focus of neo-Aristotelianism. It is on the discourse as an instrument serving the objectives of the rhetor. These objectives are taken by the neo-Aristotelian critic as they are given by the rhetor. They are not themselves the objects of appraisal. Rather, they are the stable underpinnings of the methodology. If the neo-Aristotelian critic would assess the later discourses of John C. Calhoun, and Calhoun's principle objective in these later discourses is to justify the institution of slavery, then this objective is accepted by the neo-Aristotelian critic as a standard from which the discourses can be assessed.[61] The objective itself is not evaluated, not even in its rhetorical aspects. If Calhoun's justification of slavery will condition an audience to give certain kinds of responses to other discourses, neo-Aristotelianism does not reveal this. If Calhoun's justification of slavery will mold an audience's sensibilities and, through this, work subtle alterations in linguistic conventions, neo-Aristotelianism will not tell us. To do so would require an appraisal of Calhoun's rhetorical objective, and in neo-Aristotelianism this objective is the ground of appraisal, not its object.

The general appraisal of policies advocated by rhetors is not, of course, the particular responsibility of the rhetorical critic. What shape American society would have taken had Calhoun's

---

[61] See Herbert L. Curry, "John C. Calhoun," Brigance, A History and Criticism of American Public Address, II, pp. 657–659, 661.

policies prevailed and what utility some of those policies might
have for contemporary problems can best be determined by one
with training in politics, in the social sciences, and in historiography—areas in which the rhetorician is not necessarily expert.
But the *rhetorical* appraisal of policies—that is, the estimate of
relationships between these policies and linguistic and argumentative conventions—does fall into the unique province of
rhetoric. It is an area neo-Aristotelianism leaves in mystery, because the neo-Aristotelian critic does not go beyond the objectives of the rhetor. Thus, the neo-Aristotelian critic adopts the
rhetor's ends as adequate to an assessment of the discourse, and
in this act of faith the critic equivocates on the question of what
value these ends themselves possess. That is why, though we
would probably find more objectivity in neo-Aristotelian than
in, say, literary criticism, we would also find more preoccupation with mere facts, and the exercise of lower standards, or no
standards whatever. A critical methodology that so induces its
practitioners to efface themselves and yield an essential aspect
of judicial criticism to other hands has abdicated some of its responsibility. More practically, this abdication can distort its
explication of some discourses.

A single example can illustrate the point. The "Coatesville
Address" by John Jay Chapman, delivered in 1912, is a discourse
neo-Aristotelian criticism would be hard pressed to fathom.[62]
On August 14, 1911 Chapman read in New York City newspapers an account of a particularly brutal lynching of a Negro
in Coatesville, Pennsylvania. Although he was not personally
associated in any way with the persons or place involved in the
atrocity, Chapman brooded on the event. As the first anniversary of the lynching approached, Chapman announced to his
family that he was going to Coatesville to hold a prayer meeting and to deliver a speech commemorating the terrible occasion.
In Coatesville Chapman encountered a population suspicious

---

[62] This speech has been reprinted in *American Issues*, ed. Edwin Black and
Harry P. Kerr (New York, 1961), pp. 111–114.

of his motives and growing increasingly sensitive to the approaching anniversary. After frustrating attempts to find a hall in Coatesville suitable for his meeting, Chapman finally succeeded in renting an empty store. He placed advertisements in the local paper, and held his prayer meeting on Sunday, August 18, 1912. The speech was his sermon. He delivered it to an audience of three persons: a lady friend who had accompanied him to Coatesville, an elderly Negro woman, and an unidentified man, believed to be a local spy.[63]

We are met to commemorate the anniversary of one of the most dreadful crimes in history—not for the purpose of condemning it, but to repent for our share in it. We do not start any agitation with regard to that particular crime. I understand that an attempt to prosecute the chief criminals has been made, and has entirely failed; because the whole community, and in a sense our whole people, are really involved in the guilt. The failure of the prosecution in this case, in all such cases, is only a proof of the magnitude of the guilt, and of the awful fact that everyone shares in it.

I will tell you why I am here; I will tell you what happened to me. When I read in the newspapers of August 14, a year ago, about the burning alive of a human being, and of how a few desperate, fiend-minded men had been permitted to torture a man chained to an iron bedstead, burning alive, thrust back by pitchforks when he struggled out of it, while around about stood hundreds of well-dressed American citizens, both from the vicinity and from afar, coming on foot and in wagons, assembling on telephone call, as if by magic, silent, whether from terror or indifference, fascinated and impotent, hundreds of persons watching this awful sight and making no attempt to stay the wickedness, and no one man among them all who was inspired to risk his life in an attempt to stop it, no one man to name the name of Christ, of humanity, of government! As I read the newspaper accounts of the scene enacted here in Coatesville a year ago, I seemed to get a glimpse into the unconscious soul of this country. I saw a seldom re-

---

[63] Mark A. DeWolf Howe, *John Jay Chapman and His Letters* (Boston, 1937), p. 219.

vealed picture of the American heart and of the American nature. I seemed to be looking into the heart of the criminal—a cold thing, an awful thing. I said to myself, "I shall forget this, we shall all forget it; but it will be there. What I have seen is not an illusion. It is the truth. I have seen death in the heart of this people." For to look at the agony of a fellow-being and remain aloof means death in the heart of the onlooker.

Religious fanaticism has sometimes lifted men to the frenzy of such cruelty, political passion has sometimes done it, personal hatred might do it, the excitement of the amphitheater in the degenerate days of Roman luxury could do it. But here an audience chosen by chance in America has stood spellbound through an improvised *auto-da-fé*, irregular, illegal, having no religious significance, not sanctioned by custom, having no immediate provocation, the audience standing by merely in cold dislike.

I saw during one moment something beyond all argument in the depth of its significance. You might call it the paralysis of the nerves about the heart in a people habitually and unconsciously given over to selfish aims, an ignorant people who knew not what spectacle they were providing, or what part they were playing in a judgment-play which history was exhibiting on that day.

No theories about the race problem, no statistics, legislation, or mere educational endeavor, can quite meet the lack which that day revealed in the American people. For what we saw was death. The people stood like blighted things, like ghosts about Acheron, waiting for someone or something to determine their destiny for them.

Whatever life itself is, that thing must be replenished in us. The opposite of hate is love, the opposite of cold is heat; what we need is the love of God and reverence for human nature. For one moment I knew that I had seen our true need; and I was afraid that I should forget it and that I should start schemes of education, when the need was deeper than education. And I became filled with one idea, that I must not forget what I had seen, and that I must do something to remember it. And I am here today chiefly that I may remember that vision. It seems fitting to come to this town where the crime occurred and hold a prayer-meeting, so that our hearts may be turned to God through whom mercy may flow into us.

Let me say something more about the whole matter. The subject we are dealing with is not local. The act, to be sure, took place at Coatesville and everyone looked to Coatesville to follow it up. Some months ago I asked a friend who lives not far from here something about this case, and about the expected prosecutions, and he replied to me: "It wasn't in my county," and that made me wonder whose county it was in. And it seemed to be in my county. I live on the Hudson River; but I knew that this great wickedness that happened in Coatesville is not the wickedness of Coatesville nor of today. It is the wickedness of all America and of three hundred years—the wickedness of the slave trade. All of us are tinctured by it. No special place, no special persons, are to blame. A nation cannot practice a course of inhuman crime for three hundred years and then suddenly throw off the effects of it. Less than fifty years ago domestic slavery was abolished among us; and in one way and another the marks of that vice are in our faces. There is no country in Europe where the Coatesville tragedy or anything remotely like it could have been enacted, probably no country in the world.

On the day of the calamity, those people in the automobiles came by the hundred and watched the torture, and passers-by came in a great multitude and watched it—and did nothing. On the next morning the newspapers spread the news and spread the paralysis until the whole country seemed to be helplessly watching this awful murder, as awful as anything ever done on the earth; and the whole of our people seemed to be looking on helplessly, not able to respond, not knowing what to do next. That spectacle has been in my mind.

The trouble has come down to us out of the past. The only reason slavery is wrong is that it is cruel and makes men cruel and leaves them cruel. Someone may say that you and I cannot repent because we did not do the act. But we are involved in it. We are still looking on. Do you not see that this whole event is merely the last parable, the most vivid, the most terrible illustration that ever was given by man or imagined by a Jewish prophet, of the relation between good and evil in this world, and of the relation of men to one another?

This whole matter has been an historic episode; but it is a part, not only of our national history, but of the personal history of each one of us. With the great disease (slavery) came the climax (the war), and after the climax gradually began the cure, and in the process of cure comes now the knowledge of what the evil was. I say that our need is new life, and that books and resolutions will not save us, but only such disposition in our hearts and souls as will enable the new life, love, force, hope, virtue, which surround us always, to enter into us.

This is the discovery that each man must make for him-self—the discovery that what he really stands in need of he cannot get for himself, but must wait till God gives it to him. I have felt the impulse to come here today to testify to this truth.

The occasion is not small; the occasion looks back on three centuries and embraces a hemisphere. Yet the occasion is small compared with the truth it leads us to. For this truth touches all ages and affects every soul in the world.

The verdict of neo-Aristotelianism on this speech would have to be negative. It did not fetch results. We do not know whether its hearers were impressed by the speech, but even if they were, their number was too small to matter. Further, the speech does not appear in anthologies of great orations, nor did it receive notice or acclaim after its delivery. But for a recent revival of interest in Chapman's work, it might have remained obscure indefinitely.[64] By any feasible standard of immediate effect, the speech would have to be put down as a failure.

Even the application of the Aristotelian canons cannot save the speech. In structure, the speech does sustain a mood, but there is no unfolding of a strict form. The fourth through the seventh paragraphs could be rearranged in any other order than the order in which they actually occur, and the effect would be the same. The logical supports for arguments are non-existent, as are arguments themselves, in the logical sense.

---

[64] The speech is given a paragraph's attention by Edmund Wilson in *The Triple Thinkers* (New York, 1948), p. 159. It is reported on but not reprinted in full in Howe's biography, *op cit.*, pp. 473–475. I can find no other commentary on the speech.

The main thesis, if it can be said to have one—that deliverance from Evil, of which the Coatesville atrocity was an example, can come only from God—is submitted *ex cathedra*, without a shred of proof. The emotional appeals of the speech cannot be accurately described as anger, love, fear, shame, pity, benevolence, indignation, envy, or their opposites. The ethos of the speaker, insofar as the people of Coatesville were concerned, probably consisted of the image of a fanatical crank. Chapman's solitary gesture to his immediate audience—that of seeing the crime as American rather than Coatesvillian—would hardly have been considered comforting to a group who considered themselves Americans as well as Coatesvillians. The style of the speech has the merit of vividness in its description of the lynching, but so did the newspaper accounts of the crime.

One could extend indefinitely the list of formal defects: the introduction that does not placate; the presentation of ideas embarrassing to the audience on a ceremonial occasion; the absence of a specific program or policy; the contravention of patriotic sentiments in discussing America and her people. But why go on? The speech had virtually no immediate audience anyhow, and why bother with a soliloquy that was overheard by three people? And yet, as Edmund Wilson has commented, the speech is "strange and moving." [65]

Moving it is, moving enough so that the bare calculation of its immediate effects is insufficient to account for it, moving enough so that the contemporary reader cannot feel its power as having been spent on that audience of three. The speech is not a cold marble monument. It lives. But to see its life, we must find its proper context.

The context of the Coatesville Address is not the vacant grocery store in 1912. Rather, the discourse must be understood as joining the dialogue participated in by Jefferson, Tocqueville, Lincoln, Melville, Henry Adams, Samuel Clemens, Santayana, and Faulkner—a dialogue on the moral dimension of the Amer-

---

[65] *Ibid.*

ican experience. The Coatesville Address is a particularly interesting statement in the dialogue because it is one of the very few of this century that is not cast in the form of fiction.

The context of the Coatesville Address is less a specific place than a culture, but culture in the sense that Lionel Trilling designated: "A culture is not a flow, nor even a confluence; the form of its existence is struggle, or at least debate—it is nothing if not a dialectic." [66] It is a context whose place must be measured by a continent and whose time must be reckoned in centuries. Its direct audience has been and is all of those who are interested in a meaningful interpretation of the history and moral status of this country, and indirectly its audience is all of those who are influenced by the direct audience. This dialogue has not ended, but still continues, and insofar as the model of the United States is increasingly influential in other parts of the world, the potential audience to this dialogue grows larger.

Our warrant for taking the context of the Coatesville Address so broadly is suggested by Chapman himself. The first two paragraphs insistently demand that his auditors focus, not on Coatesville, but on the country. His very first idea is that "our whole people are involved in the guilt." From there he talks of "American citizens . . . of the American heart and of the American nature." Later he makes it explicit: ". . . this great wickedness that happened in Coatesville is not the wickedness of Coatesville nor of today. It is the wickedness of all America and of three hundred years . . ."

So much for context. Next we must consider what the speech actually says. It is, most obviously, an interpretation of an event. The event, of course, is the lynching of the preceding year. Reduced to its manifest essentials, the event is the killing of a Negro by a group of whites. That would be the simplest way of describing it; but hardly anyone then, and hardly anyone

---

[66] Lionel Trilling, "Reality in America," *Literary Opinion in America*, ed. Morton Dauwen Zabel, 3rd ed., rev. (New York and Evanston, Ill., 1962), p. 408.

now, could perceive the event so simply. Our perceptions of the event will be colored by our moral dispositions. Hence, there would conceivably be those who would perceive the event as a righteous act of vengeful justice; there would be those who would perceive it as a hideous expression of mob violence; there would be those who would perceive it, clinically, as the concrete illustration of an abstract sociopathic idea; there would be those who would refuse to perceive the event at all, who would dismiss it and put it out of mind.

This range of reactions does not exhaust the possibilities. Indeed, the possibilities are, in a sense, inexhaustible, for we must always allow the possibility of someone's perceiving the event with a singular collocation of responses drawn from his personal history; but these are the most conspicuous reactions, and, because they are most conspicuous, they would also probably be the most popular ones. Of these four reactions, we can infer that Chapman regarded the first and last of them as wrong, and the second and third of them as requiring emendation. The function of his speech was to provide this emendation—to shape the appropriate reaction to the event.

We must look to the speech for verification of this inference. Chapman makes no allowance for the defensibility of the first response, which would constitute approval of the event. He does not assume—he probably could not conceive of—an auditor to his speech regarding the event as a righteous act. His description of the killers "desperate, fiend-minded men"—and his description of the event—"burning alive of a human being . . . wickedness . . . the heart of the criminal"—presuppose disapproval of the event. He who would applaud the event is not a part of Chapman's audience, by Chapman's own choice.

The fourth of our responses—indifference to the event—is explicitly repudiated by Chapman: ". . . it seemed to be in my county. . . . It is the wickedness of all America . . . All of us are tinctured by it . . . it is a part, not only of our national history, but of the personal history of each one of us." Chapman recognizes the possibility of an initial reaction of indifference (for example, his friend who said, "It wasn't in my county"), but Chapman's argument on the national guilt for the event renders passive indifference impossible. One who, having read his speech, would remain detached from the event would have to deny his responsibility for the killing, and by the very act of denial he would enter into a relationship with the event. His reaction could not longer be passively indifferent because his act of denial would itself betoken a connection with the event. Admittedly, it would be a negative connection—the denial of a connection—but not even this denial could be made without a focus on the relationship between the auditor and the event. Chapman's speech forces the auditor to perceive the event and to examine his own relationship to it; hence, the speech undermines the possibility of passive indifference.

Of the second and third responses—the outraged response and the clinical response—Chapman's speech combines and emends the two. We can infer that neither of these responses is singly acceptable to Chapman. Outrage is unacceptable because it represents an excess of moral zeal; didacticism is unacceptable because it represents a deficiency of moral zeal. Chapman's effort is to combine the two in such a way that the event is perceived with moral color but at the same time perceived with perspective. We are here confronting a fine and delicate balance requiring patient exposition.

Let us look more closely at the outraged response. Let us, in fact, consider what would constitute a case of ideal outrage. Would it not be the case of one who would seize his own pitchfork and push the killers into the fire? Is not punishment the characteristic satisfaction of outrage? And further, to be truly satisfying, does not this punishment have, in some way, to fit the crime—that is, to be as severe in its way as the crime was? The practical expression of outrage is the invocation of the Mosaic Law. We need look no further than Coatesville to see the relationship illustrated, for the man who was lynched was suspected of murder. His own murder by the lynch mob was no more than an equivalent act, and it does not strain our credulity to imagine the Coatesville mob claiming the sanction of justice in the midst of their sanguinary business. Thus, the outraged response to the Coatesville affair would be merely a perpetuation of the response that led to the affair in the first place. Outrage, with its concomitant thirst for revenge, would be morally indistinguishable from the crime itself.

And what of the alternative reaction—the clinical perception of the event as a concrete illustration of an abstract idea? Here we see another extreme, for this perception of the event, though it would promote the composure of poised tranquility, would approach indifference in its moral concern. The clinical attitude has no moral counterpart; it paralyzes action. If vengeance is the practical expression of outrage, then acquiescence is the practical expression of didacticism. And we must further consider that the very sensibility required by didacticism can be destroyed by it, "for to look at the agony of a fellow-being and remain aloof means death in the heart of the onlooker."

Chapman thus shapes a perception of the lynching that moderates outrage with detachment, moderates it, in fact, so extensively that it is substantively transformed and becomes a reaction for which we have no precise word in English. We do not need a word so long as we have Chapman's speech, for it enables us to experience the reaction. We are his audience.

Chapman would have us perceive the event as a scene in a morality play. The play itself is the history of this country, seen as the death-through-sin and the potential rebirth-through-purification of a whole people. The issues of crime and punishment, of blame and defense, would not shape the auditor's response, just as they do not shape it in a tragic drama. The lynching is seen as a ritual murder, and the appropriate response to it is a religious experience. We are able, through this response, to view the lynching unequivocally as a crime, and yet we do not hate the criminals, for we feel ourselves to be responsible. The net practical effect of the speech on the thoroughly attentive auditor is to make him incapable of lynching —incapable because, instead of being aware of a specific and singular case, he has become aware of the moral nature of lynching. He has, in sum, not simply a moral reaction, but a moral insight.

And how are we to appraise the speech? First, we must reiterate that the speech still lives. That is, it addresses itself to the contemporary auditor. Its point of view is not transitory; it is not a product of the historical moment; it is not a collection of rhetorical tactics. The speech is built upon settled conclusions regarding the nature of men and their world, the history and destiny of a country, and it is this solid foundation that makes for its persistent viability. The speech is a symptom of an intricately moral interpretation of American history. It is the token of a complex of judgments, attitudes, and discriminations so manifested that the auditor is passed beyond the surface of the discourse and confronts its resonant implications. The passage of time, therefore, can only enable the audiences to this speech to apprehend its ramifications, to discern the range of its applicability, to explicate its complexities and absorb its overtones.

There is also a historical accident—or perhaps it is a historical inevitability—that will work to guarantee its continued life. That is the loss of innocence in America. Chapman's audience is primarily his countrymen, and this audience has grown better able to understand the Coatesville Address since 1912. We have endured two world wars, we have destroyed cities, we have felt the temptations of empire, and we have seen the fall of the god Progress. We are not the innocent children of 1912, and though we may not be wiser than our grandfathers, we are certainly less confident of our rectitude. Hence, it may be that Chapman's Coatesville Address is only just now finding its understanding audience, and it may be that that audience will grow larger and more attentive with every passing day. We can surmise a future for this speech: a future of influence in shaping our perception, not just of a crime committed in 1911, but of the sort of crime for which this century has had a special proclivity.

Moreover, our generation seems to have an appetite for guilt, one that the Coatesville Address tends to gratify. The causes of this appetite are obscure, but whatever the reason for it, it is there—so that we are greedy for the books of our alien critics and savor every flagellation, and we brood and debate upon where we went wrong as a nation and what we should do to set things right again. Insofar as the Coatesville Address treats of national guilt, that speech should increasingly find its audience.

And yet another attainment: the speech preserves a morally significant event; it makes it permanent in history—timeless. By shaping a perception, instead of merely re-creating an incident as a newsreel camera might, the speech makes available to the future the experience of a sensitive mind in converse with an objective occurrence that has struck that mind as morally critical. It is through the speech that we know the moral crisis, and by the speech that we are persuaded of it. This, again, is because the speech shapes a perception; it does not neutrally record. In functioning in this way, in conveying an experience that is unique for almost all its auditors and thus opening to them a new possibility for subsequent experience and creating in them a new potentiality for perceiving subsequent events, the speech shares, in its more modest way, a quality of the supreme works of our literature.

Our appraisal of the Coatesville Address must be high. The most convincing gesture of evidence for this appraisal would be to point to the speech. But beyond the speech, confirming our approval, is its capacity for continuing to live as an influence, and for illuminating many of those aspects of our national experience with which we are most concerned.

Finally, there is the strongest confirmation of all: the vision of the fullest rhetorical potentialities of the speech. Insofar as we can imagine an auditor who yields himself completely to its influence, we can see one who would be delivered from the conflict of niggling ideologies. He would be moral without being righteous, passionate without being violent. He would be a reformer of the spirit, whose domain of responsibility would extend to all men everywhere.

It is a tragic irony that the life of John Jay Chapman illustrated the very *harmatia* that he saw most clearly at Coatesville. Four years after the speech was given, Chapman's son was killed in the First World War, and Chapman gave rabid expression to his agony in anti-German pamphlets. Afterwards he slipped into parochialism: Boston and the affairs of Harvard were the center of his universe; anti-Semitism and anti-Catholicism poured out of him, and Chapman, half mad, sank into death, hating. It is Chapman at Coatesville who gives us the measure of his own tragedy, a tragedy wherein the anti-ideologue falls victim to ideology; the man who would transcend hate dies a hater.

We can even see in Chapman's later surrender to vindictiveness how triumphant was his sublimation of it at Coatesville. The tendency toward it was already a strong force in him— other aspects of his life bear this out—and it held for him a terrible attraction, so that the seed of his insight and the seed of his destruction were the same seed. Yet, for a few minutes at least, in a vacant grocery store in an obscure Pennsylvania town, the diverse convictions of John Jay Chapman came together in such a way as to open to him the darker recesses of our society; and his response to that disclosure, as well as the particular convergence of his values that made it possible, are imperishably preserved in his speech.

It will suffice for the present to observe that a system of rhetorical criticism that can give no satisfactory accounting of an excellent work—as neo-Aristotelianism can give no accounting of the Coatesville Address—is seriously compromised as a critical system. And the critic who is obliged by the nature of his theories to yield to the judgment of those who may be less qualified than he to judge little qualifies as a critic so long as he suffers those theories to guide him.

CHAPTER IV

Aristotle and
Rhetorical Criticism

IN DEALING WITH a critical methodology derived from Aristotle, our concern is quite properly with what Aristotle has been taken to mean by his modern disciples rather than with what Aristotle may actually have meant. There is no end to perfecting our texts of the ancients or to the just ascription of meaning to those texts. But the echo of a sound can sometimes acquire more stability than the original, and in investigating neo-Aristotelian- ism in rhetorical criticism, we are dealing with an echo.

The uses that have actually been made of Aristotle's *Rhetoric* are by no means identical with the uses the *Rhetoric* will allow. The entire section on style, for example, because its generaliza- tions are founded on the Greek language, is largely ignored by modern rhetorical critics. And many another passage in our text of Aristotle has been transmuted in its modern application to the criticism of rhetorical discourse. Indeed, this very application itself is probably alien to the conceptions of Aristotle, since there is no evidence in the *Rhetoric* that its generalizations were intended for the appraisal of rhetorical discourses.

The relationship of a derivative set of critical conventions to its textual source is likely to be highly complicated. In neo-Aristotelianism, we do not find literal application of principles in the *Rhetoric*, precisely because literal interpretation of the *Rhetoric* is itself so problematical a subject. What we do find in neo-Aristotelianism is a point of view, an approach, and, perhaps most manifestly, a circumscription of subject matter whose counterparts can be found in the original text. Just as an echo is, to some degree, a distortion of the sound that is its source, so neo-Aristotelian criticism has altered and transformed the ideas that are its source. We cannot expect an echo to reproduce its source with absolute fidelity, but we do expect that the tone and duration of the echo will be determined by the initial sound. In the same way, the reverberations of Aristotle's work, passing through all the distortions of two thousand years of commentary, will still retain some residue of the original, even in the variations neo-Aristotelian critics play upon those antique themes. Thus, in inquiring into the scope of neo-Aristotelian criticism, we do well to begin by considering the scope of Aristotle's own work in rhetoric. Aristotle will not answer for neo-Aristotelianism, but Aristotle may help to explain it.

Aristotle had a characteristic manner of seeing human enterprises, both in their individual integrity and in their relations to one another. To him, every human activity was directed toward some end, drawn to some final cause or culmination. And each end, in its turn, was regarded by him as serving some higher end, until, under the aspect of all human effort, one finally came to see the ends of all activities arranged in a hierarchy and culminating in a single supreme end; so that every activity, every art and every science, had a state of fruition that was ultimate for it, but that, in broader perspective, subserved yet higher activities with higher ends. Summarily, such is the picture of purposive conduct that we are presented by Aristotle.

In determining the scope of Aristotle's theory of rhetoric, we must confront the question of how we are to take the word *krisis*, translated as *judgment*, in two crucial passages of the *Rhetoric* in which Aristotle seems to make explicit pronouncements about the end of rhetoric. The passages in question, with the critical terms italicized, are

> But since the object of Rhetoric is *judgement*—for judgements are pronounced in deliberative rhetoric and *judicial proceedings* are a *judgement* . . .[1]

Now the employment of persuasive speeches is directed towards a *judgement* . . . speaking generally, he who has to be persuaded is a *judge* . . . the epideictic speech is put together with reference to the spectator as if he were a *judge* . . . only he who decides questions at issue in civil controversies is a judge in the proper sense of the word . . .[2]

Cope's commentary on these two passages is suggestive, although Cope gives no indication that he is aware of the ambiguity of the English word judgment. Of the first passage above, Cope notes that the signification of *krisis* and its variants has been extended "to include decisions or *judgements* of all kinds, moral, political, . . . literary . . . as well as the ordinary application of it to the judicial decisions of the judges in a court of law . . ."[3]

Of the second passage above, Cope writes:

> All speeches which have persuasion for their object are addressed to, or look to, a *decision* of some kind. In the two more important branches of Rhetoric, the deliberative and forensic, . . . the *decision* and the *judge* may be understood literally: in the third or epideictic branch, the

---

[1] Aristotle, *The "Art" of Rhetoric*, John Henry Freese, trans. (London and New York, 1926), 1377b, 21–22. Unless otherwise specified, all quotations from the *Rhetoric* will be from Freese's Loeb Library edition, Harvard University Press.

[2] *Ibid.*, 1391b, 8.

[3] Edward Meredith Cope, *The Rhetoric of Aristotle with a Commentary*, ed. John Edwin Sandys (Cambridge, England, 1877), vol. II, p. 2.

audience is in some sense also a judge, in his capacity of
critic, being called upon to *decide* or pass sentence on the
merits of the composition. Still it is only in the first two
that the term "judge" can be applied to the hearer in its
absolute, or strict and proper sense . . .[4]

Inasmuch as the end of rhetorical activity was conceived by
Aristotle to be something his modern translators take to be
accurately rendered by the English word judgment, it becomes
vitally important for us to understand what *judgment* means in
order to gain some insight into the scope of Aristotle's view of
rhetoric. Unfortunately for our present purposes, *judgment* is
used in more than one sense in the English language, and the
exact sense in which Aristotle can be taken is not revealed in
the passages from the *Rhetoric* cited above. Further, Cope appears not to have focussed on this ambiguity either in the specific
comments quoted above or in his general explication of the
Rhetoric. The ambiguity itself can be illuminated by recourse to
the *Oxford English Dictionary*. This source lists a number of
different usages of *judgment*, some of which are obviously immaterial to Aristotle's meaning, as, for example, the use in the
phrase "last judgment." The definitions that might have relevance to Aristotle are (1) "The action of trying a cause in a
court of justice; trial"; (2) "The sentence of a court of justice; a
judicial decision or order in court"; (3) "Any formal or authoritative decision, as of an umpire or arbiter"; (4) "The pronounc-
ing of a deliberate opinion upon a person or thing, or the opinion
pronounced; criticism; censure"; (5) "The formation of an
opinion or notion concerning something by exercising the mind
upon it; an opinion, estimate"; (6) "The faculty of judging;
ability to form an opinion; that function of the mind whereby
it arrives at a notion of anything; the critical faculty; discern-
ment." [5]

For the convenience of further discussion of Aristotle's mean-

---

[4] *Ibid.*, vol. II, p. 174.
[5] All quotations are from the *Oxford English Dictionary* (Oxford, England,
1933), V, pp. 618–619.

ing we can consolidate these definitions of judgment into three general usages: judgment as a faculty, judgment as a process, and judgment as an object. We use the term judgment to refer to a faculty or capacity in such expressions as "a man of sound judgment." We are referring to some innate combination of moral and intellectual qualities that enables a person to render fair and sound decisions. We use the term to refer to a process in such expressions as "biased judgment," where we would be referring to a procedure or method that went wrong. We use the term to refer to an object in such expressions as "the judgment was that the defendant was guilty." Here we refer to no more than the actual decision rendered, irrespective of any faculty the judge may have exercised or any procedure he may have followed. We must further note of the term judgment, that, like most ambiguous words, it may, in a given context, entail or imply more than one of its possible meanings. Although the three usages of judgment are distinct, they are not necessarily mutually exclusive. For example, the sentence, "Sound judgment was exercised upon the case at issue," clearly refers to the *faculty* of judgment, but the sentence also implies something about the process and the object as well. Consequently, we must posit a fourth general category: the ambiguous, in which the term judgment refers or seems to refer to more than one of its three possible referents. With this brief examination of judgment before us, we can better review Aristotle's usage of *krisis* in order to determine the sense in which Aristotle used the term and, subsequent to that determination, to discover more exactly his meaning in the two passages quoted above. To make for easier reference, the passages in Aristotle in which *krisis* and its variants appear will be numbered.[6] In each passage the English word that renders *krisis* or any of its variants will be italicized.

1) . . . the faction at Heraclea and that at Thebes arose out of *judgment* of a law court, when the people at Hera-

---

[6] The passages were obtained through the use of Herman Bonitz's *Index Aristotelicus* (Berlin, 1870). I have listed all passages recorded by Bonitz in which I was able to find *krisis*.

clea justly but factiously enforced the punishment against Eurytion on a charge of adultery and those at Thebes did so against Archias . . .[7]

2) . . . the law about *trials* is unsatisfactory—the impression for a qualified *verdict* though the charge in the indictment is unqualified, and the conversion of the juror into an arbitrator.[8]

Barker's rendering of this passage is: "We may also disagree with the law he proposes in regard to the method of giving *judicial decisions*. He prescribes that a judge (if he thinks fit) give a qualified *verdict* . . ."[9]

3) He held that the *verdicts* in the courts ought not to be given by ballot . . .[10]

4) Another magistracy is the one that has to receive a written return of private contracts and of the *verdicts* of the law courts . . .[11]

5) . . . the existence of certain pleasures which are base has been another ground for this *belief* that Pleasure is no good thing.[12]

6) Another method is to appeal to a *verdict* already given . . . his accuser did wrong in transferring the *decisions* of the court of Dionysus to the law courts . . .[13]

7) The fourth kind of objection is derived from the former *decisions* of well-known men. For instance, if the enthymeme is that one should make allowances for those who are drunk, for their offence is the result of ignorance, it may be objected that Pittacus then is unworthy of commendation, otherwise he would not have laid down severer punishment for a man who commits an offence when drunk.[14]

---

[7] Aristotle, *Politics*, H. Rackham, trans. (London, 1959), 1306a, 37.

[8] *Ibid.*, 1268b, 5.

[9] Ernest Barker, trans. *The Politics of Aristotle* (Oxford, England, 1946).

[10] Aristotle, *Politics*, H. Rackham, trans. (London, 1959), 1268a, 1.

[11] *Ibid.*, 1321b, 35.

[12] Aristotle, *Magna Moralia*, G. Cyril Armstrong, trans. (London, 1958), 1205a, 28.

[13] Aristotle, *Rhetoric*, 1416a, 35.

[14] *Ibid.*, 1402b, 8.

8) Another topic is that from a previous *judgement* in regard to the same or a similar or contrary matter . . . of
the *judges* themselves . . . or of those whose *judgement*
they accept . . .[15]

9) . . . it is proper that laws . . . should themselves define the issue of all cases . . . and leave as little as possible
to the discretion of the *judges* . . . *judgements* are delivered on the spur of the moment, so that it is difficult for
the judges properly to *decide* questions of justice or
expediency . . .[16]

10) . . . the member of the public assembly and the dicast
have to *decide* present and definite issues, and in their case
love, hate, or personal interest is often involved, so that
they are no longer capable of discerning the truth adequately, their *judgement* being obscured by their own
pleasure or pain.[17]

Cooper's rendering of the final clause is ". . . their *judgment*
clouded by their own pleasure or pain." [18] Rhys Roberts renders
it: ". . . have their *judgement* obscured by considerations of
personal pleasure or pain." [19]

11) . . . these [persons who enjoy being honored by good
men] like honour because they are assured of their worth
by their confidence in the *judgment* of those who assert
it.[20]

12) And the bestowal of a share in the government upon
the multitude would go on the lines stated before . . . or
as at Marseilles, by making a *selection* among members of
the governing classes and those outside it of persons who
deserve inclusion.[21]

---

[15] *Ibid.*, 1398b, 12–19.
[16] *Ibid.*, 1354a.
[17] *Ibid.*, 1354b.
[18] Lane Cooper, trans., *The Rhetoric of Aristotle* (New York, 1932), p. 2.
[19] W. Rhys Roberts, trans., *Aristotle's Rhetoric* (New York, 1954), p. 21.
[20] Aristotle, *Nicomachean Ethics*, H. Rackham, trans. (London, 1926), 1159a, 24.
[21] Aristotle, *Politics*, 1321a, 30.

13) Again, the procedure in the selection of the Elders as a mode of *selection* is not only childish, but it is also wrong . . .[22]

14) A citizen pure and simple is defined by nothing else so much as by the right to participate in *judicial functions* and in office.[23]

15) . . . they *judge* a great state by the numerical magnitude of the population, but really the more proper thing to look at is not members but efficiency.[24]

16) . . . and most necessary [occupation] of all, a provision for *deciding* questions of interest and of rights between citizens.[25]

17) . . . the Ephors have *jurisdiction* in lawsuits of high importance, although they are any chance people, so that it would be better if they did not *decide* cases on their own judgement [Barker has "at discretion"] but by written rules and according to the laws.[26]

18) For taste is concerned with *discriminating* flavours . . .[27]

19) Between persons of the same kind *discrimination* is comparatively easy . . .[28]

20) It is therefore not easy to pronounce on principle what degree and manner of error is blameworthy, since this is a matter of the particular circumstances and *judgment* rests with the faculty of perception.[29]

21) . . . the administration of the law means the *discrimination* of what is just and what is unjust.[30]

22) . . . accuracy in *distinguishing* the differences both of

---

[22] *Ibid.*, 1271a, 10.
[23] *Ibid.*, 1271a, 10.
[24] *Ibid.*, 1326a, 14.
[25] *Ibid.*, 1328a, 14.
[26] *Ibid.*, 1270b, 28.
[27] Aristotle, *Nicomachean Ethics*, 1118a, 28.
[28] *Ibid.*, 1165a, 34.
[29] *Ibid.*, 1126b, 4.
[30] *Ibid.*, 1134a, 31.

sounds and smells depends upon the purity of the sense-organ . . .[31]

23) He therefore appointed a tribunal and made proclamation that all who failed to appear before it within a stated period should lose the right to a legal *decision* of their outstanding claims.[32]

24) The same process can be *detected* in olives . . .[33]

25) . . . touch is the *test* of existence for the tangible.[34]

26) . . . there is no discussion, so the *judgement* is clear.[35]

Freese notes: "The meaning apparently is that there is no discussion, as might be the case when there were several judges, so that the decision is clear and unbiased . . ." [36] Jebb renders it: ". . . the turmoil is absent, so that the *judgement* is serene . . ." [37] And in a note: "unclouded." [38] Cooper's rendering: ". . . there being no actual contest, his *judgment* is uncontaminated." [39] Rhys Roberts' rendering: ". . . the struggle is less intense and so the *judgement* is undisturbed." [40]

27) . . . their life-tenure in the *judgeship* is indeed a questionable feature . . .[41]

---

[31] Aristotle, *Generation of Animals*, A. L. Peck, trans. (London, 1953), 781b, 2.

[32] Aristotle, *Oeconomica*, G. Cyril Armstrong, trans. (London, 1958), 1348b, 13.

[33] Aristotle, *On Plants*, W. S. Hett, trans. (London, 1955), 827a, 39.

[34] Aristotle, *Physics*, Philip H. Wicksteed and Francis M. Cornford, trans. (London, 1929), 216b, 19.

[35] Aristotle, *Rhetoric*, 1414a, 14.

[36] *Ibid.*, pp. 422–423.

[37] Richard C. Jebb, trans. *The Rhetoric of Aristotle* (Cambridge, England, 1909).

[38] *Ibid.*

[39] Lane Cooper, trans., *The Rhetoric of Aristotle* (New York, 1932), p. 219.

[40] Rhys Roberts, *op. cit.*, p. 198.

[41] Aristotle, *Politics*, 1270b, 39.

Barker's rendering: ". . . whether councillors should be life judges in important *cases* . . ." [42] Jowett's rendering: ". . . judges of important *causes* . . ." [43]

28) As it is, the citizens assembled hear lawsuits and deliberate and give *judgements*, but these *judgements* are all on particular cases.[44]

29) In Arcadia . . . one of the inhabitants was brought into *court* . . .[45]

30) . . . for a formed judgement is stable and not doing things quickly or easily makes the *judgement* right.[46]

31) The emotions are all those affections which cause men to change their opinion in regard to their *judgements* and are accompanied by pleasure and pain . . .[47]

Cooper's rendering: "By these, the emotions, are meant those states which are attended by pain and pleasure, and which, as they change, make a difference in our *judgments* (of the same thing) . . ." [48] Rhys Roberts' rendering: "The Emotions are all those feelings that so change men as to affect their *judgements*, and that are also attended by pain or pleasure." [49] Cope notes: ". . . 'are brought over to a different state of mind or feeling . . . in respect of their decisions,' of *all* kinds; but especially judicial decisions and those of national assemblies on questions of policy or expediency." [50]

If we apply to these passages the general categories for judgment that we have derived from the *Oxford English Dictionary*

[42] Barker, *op. cit.*

[43] Benjamin Jowett, trans. *Aristotle's Politics* (Oxford, England, 1905).

[44] Aristotle, *Politics*, H. Rackham, trans. (London, 1959), 1286a, 27.

[45] Aristotle, *Parts of Animals*, A. L. Peck, trans. (London, 1937), 673a, 18.

[46] Aristotle, *Eudemian Ethics*, H. Rackham, trans. (London, 1952), 1237b, 12.

[47] Aristotle, *Rhetoric*, 1378a, 21.

[48] Cooper, *op. cit.*, p. 92.

[49] Roberts, *op. cit.*, pp. 91–92.

[50] Edward Meredith Cope, *The Rhetoric of Aristotle with a Commentary*, ed. John Edwin Sandys (Cambridge, England, 1877), vol. II, p. 7.

—namely, object, faculty, process, and ambiguity, we can see that Aristotle's uses of *krisis* and its variants fall into the same classifications. Passages 1 through 9 seem most clearly to employ the term as an object. Passages 10 and 11 seem to refer to a faculty. Passages 12 through 26 seem to refer to a process. Passages 27 through 31 must be regarded as ambiguous. As we might have expected, the classification of each passage is not clear-cut. Passage 30, for example, is listed as ambiguous because it is not really clear whether the judgment that is to be made "right" is the decision (object) or the adjudication (process). In the case of the term judgment, such a distinction is unnecessary, because a usage of the term that entailed both object and process is perfectly legitimate. What we seem to have in the passages cited is evidence that the same rule of usage applies to *krisis*. In passage 30 we have the ambiguous usage, but the context clearly implies a process of judging by suggesting a rule or requisite of procedure that would insure the rightness of the judgment.

Similarly in passage 8, the first judgment seems to refer to a precedent-making decision, a judgment as object; the use of the second judgment in the same passage strongly suggests, however, the faculty of judging rather than the object of judgment. Cope's commentary on this section completes the ambiguity by discussing standards that can only be applicable to the process of judging.

> We have here . . . a classification of "authorities" from whose foregone decisions we may draw an inference as to the truth of a statement or the rectitude of a principle, act, or course of policy . . . Such are . . . the good, the right-minded, and therefore sound judging; whose minds are unclouded by passion or partiality, unbiased by prejudice, clear to decide aright: men of [practical wisdom] who have *acquired the habit* of right judgment in practical business and moral distinctions.[51]

---

[51] Cope, *op. cit.*, p. 264.

We would have to regard this note of Cope's, together with passages 10, 13, 17, 20, and 26, as definitive in indicating a usage in Aristotle of *krisis* and its variants to refer to more than simply a decision—the object of the adjudicatory process. These passages quite clearly employ the terms to mean other than a decision, and they are especially cited because their departure from the object sense of *krisis* is unmistakable. Cope's note, in calling attention to a characteristic procedure of Aristotle's moral and political writings, further confirms that Aristotle must have had in his mind a conception of a process of judging.

Other students of Greek have employed *krisis* and its variants in the same ways in which we now employ the English word judgment. Quintilian, for example, is clearly using the term in its sense of referring to an object in this passage:

> Authority also may be drawn from external sources to support a case. Those who follow the Greeks, who call such arguments *kriseis*, style them *judgments* or *adjudications*, thereby referring not to matters on which judicial sentence has been pronounced (for such decisions form examples or precedents), but to whatever may be regarded as expressing the opinion of nations, peoples, philosophers, distinguished citizens, or illustrious poets.[52]

Housman, in his polemical introduction to his edition of Juvenal, employs the term to refer to a process, and a process that meets certain standards and obeys certain rules of procedure: "If you suppose yourself able to distinguish a true reading from a false one, —suppose yourself, that is, to be a critic, a man capable of doing what the Greeks called *krinein* . . ."[53]

What is most striking about the passages from Aristotle, the commentary of Cope, the quotations from Quintilian and Housman, is how similar *krisis* is to the English *judgment*. Every major variation in the meaning of *judgment* seems to

---

[52] Quintilian, *Institutio Oratoria*, H. E. Butler, trans. (London, 1921), vol. V, bk. xi, p. 36.

[53] D. Ivnii Ivvenalis, *Satvrae*, ed. A. E. Housman (London, 1931), p. xii.

have its counterpart in the Greek term. And what is most pertinent to our present inquiry is that these variations in *krisis* were obviously known to Aristotle, since he employed them. When, with this information in mind, we return to the two questionable passages from the *Rhetoric* that were quoted earlier, we are given pause. What can it mean to say that "the object of Rhetoric is judgment?" Or "the employment of persuasive speeches is directed towards a judgment?" Would Aristotle have expressed himself in this way if all that he meant to refer to was the decision finally rendered by the judicial audience, or the policy finally endorsed by the deliberative audience? Our evidence negates this last question. We have, first, the fact that Aristotle more often used *krisis* to refer to a process of judging than to an object of judgment. Second, we have the fact that, if Aristotle had only meant to say that persuasive discourse culminated or found its end in an audience's believing something, Aristotle had clearer and more direct terms available to him for expressing such a meaning.

First there is *doxa*, which Bonitz finds Aristotle repeatedly using to mean notion or opinion.[54] Below are passages in which Aristotle uses this term and its variants to mean opinion. The first passage quoted is Aristotle's definition and analysis of the term.

But the only things that are true are intuition, knowledge and *opinion*, and the discourse resulting from these. Therefore we are left with the conclusion that it is *opinion* that is concerned with that which is true or false and which may be otherwise. In other words *opinion* is the assumption of a premiss which is neither mediated nor necessary. This description agrees with observed usage; for *opinion*, like events of the character which we have just described, is uncertain. Besides, no one thinks that he is "*opining*" when he thinks that a thing cannot be otherwise; he thinks that he has knowledge. It is when he thinks that a thing is so, but nevertheless there is no reason why it should not be

---

54 Hermann Bonitz, *Index Aristotelicus* (Berlin, 1870), pp. 203–204.

otherwise, that he thinks that he is *opining;* which implies that *opinion* is concerned with this sort of proposition, while knowledge is concerned with that which must be so.
. . . it is impossible to have *opinion* and knowledge at the same time about the same object; otherwise one would apprehend that the same thing both could and could not be otherwise, which is impossible. Knowledge and *opinion* of the same object may exist separately in different minds in the sense which we have explained; but they cannot so exist in the same mind.[55]

But judgments which a man passes in accordance with his personal *opinion,* even if they are false, are valid in the eyes of the law . . .[56]

. . . there is no reason why any judgement which is given in accordance with the judge's *opinion* should not be just.[57]

The two passages immediately preceding are especially interesting in that they explicitly contrast the term with *krisis.*

Yet it seems that knowledge and perception and *opinion* and understanding are always of something else, and only incidentally of themselves.[58]

But to attach equal importance to the *opinions* and impressions of disputing parties is foolish because clearly one side or the other must be wrong.[59]

One may be of *opinion* [sic], and truly, that such or such a person is sitting. And yet, when that person has risen, that opinion, if held still, is false.[60]

Indeed, the popular *opinion* about the way in which un-

---

[55] Aristotle, *Posterior Analytics,* E. S. Forster, trans. (London, 1950), 89a.
[56] Aristotle, *On Sophistical Refutations,* E. S. Forster, trans. (London, 1955), 180b, 24.
[57] *Ibid.,* 180b, 33.
[58] Aristotle, *Metaphysics,* Hugh Tredennick, trans. (London, 1956), 1075a, 36.
[59] *Ibid.,* 1062b, 33.
[60] Aristotle, *The Categories,* Harold P. Cooke, trans. (London, 1938), 4a, 23.

qualified coming-to-be and passing-away occur, differs from the truth . . .[61]

"Choice" is "taking," but not taking simply—it is taking one thing in preference to another; but this cannot be done without consideration and deliberation; hence purposive choice arises out of deliberative *opinion*.[62]

. . . demogogues owe their rise to greatness to the fact that the people is sovereign over all things while they are sovereign over the *opinion* of the people, for the multitude believes them.[63]

. . . wisdom assuredly is not a subject's virtue, but only right *opinion* . . .[64]

Nor yet is Deliberative Excellence any form of *Opinion*. But inasmuch as a bad deliberator makes mistakes and a good deliberator deliberates correctly, it is clear that Deliberative Excellence is some form of correctness; though it is not correctness of Knowledge, nor of *Opinion*. Correctness cannot be predicated of Knowledge, any more than can error, and correctness of *Opinion* is truth; and also any matter about which one has an *opinion* has been settled already; . . . for *Opinion* has passed beyond the stage of investigation and is a form of affirmation, whereas a man deliberating, whether he deliberates well or badly, is investigating and calculating something.[65]

It seems that anything may be matter of *opinion*—we form *opinions* about what is eternal, or impossible, just as much as about what is within our power. Also we distinguish *opinion* by its truth or falsehood, not by its being good or bad. Probably therefore nobody actually identifies choice with *opinion* in general. But neither is it the same as some

---

[61] Aristotle, *On Coming-to-Be and Passing-Away*, E. S. Forster, trans. (London, 1945), 318b, 27.

[62] Aristotle, *Eudemian Ethics*, H. Rackham, trans. (London, 1952), 1226b, 9.

[63] Aristotle, *Politics*, H. Rackham, trans. (London, 1959), 1292a, 27.

[64] *Ibid.*, 1277b, 28.

[65] Aristotle, *Nicomachean Ethics*, H. Rackham, trans. (London, 1926), 1142b, 6–17.

particular *opinion*. For it is our choice of good or evil that determines our character, not our *opinion* about good or evil. And we choose to take or avoid some good or evil thing, but we *opine* what a thing is, or for whom it is advantageous, or how it is so: we do not exactly form an *opinion* to take or avoid a thing. And we choose only things that we absolutely know to be good, we *opine* things we do not quite certainly know to be true. Nor do the same persons appear to excel both at choosing and at forming *opinions*: some people seem to form *opinions* better, but yet to choose the wrong things from wickedness. That choice is preceded or accompanied by the formation of an *opinion* is immaterial, for that is not the point we are considering, but whether choice is the same thing as some form of *opinion*.[66]

Of the two parts of the soul possessed of reason, Prudence must be the virtue of one, namely, the part that forms *opinions*; for *Opinion* deals with that which can vary, and so does Prudence.[67]

Finally, we may examine some appearances of the term *doxa* in the *Rhetoric* itself. The first passage below is especially noteworthy inasmuch as it also contains a variant of *pistis*, which, as shall subsequently be argued, was another term available to Aristotle had he wished to say that persuasive discourse finds its end in belief or conviction.

. . . such are the *opinions* and propositions that are useful to produce conviction [*pisteis*] in these circumstances.[68]

Now, since each kind of Rhetoric as was said, has its own special end, and in regard to all of them we have gathered popular *opinions* and premises whence men derive their proofs . . .[69]

And the objection is not an enthymeme, but . . . it is

---

[66] *Ibid.*, 1111b, 30–1112a, 13.
[67] *Ibid.*, 1140b, 27.
[68] Aristotle, *Rhetoric*, 1377b, 18.
[69] *Ibid.*, 1391b, 24.

stating an *opinion* which is intended to make it clear that the adversary's syllogism is not logical . . .[70]

For, as we have said, before friends we do not blush for faults merely condemned by public *opinion* . . .[71]

. . . not one heeds the *opinion* of others except on account of those who hold it . . .[72]

Plato, whose lectures Aristotle attended for over two decades, repeatedly employed the term to refer to the object of persuasion. Plato is quite explicit on the matter as, for example, when he causes Socrates to ask: "And persuading them is making them have an *opinion*, is it not?" [73] Again, in the *Timaeus*, when Plato is at pains to draw a distinction between Reason, which is the result of teaching, and True Opinion, which is the result of persuasion, the term that is rendered as Opinion is *doxa*.[74]

Another term employed by both Plato and Aristotle to mean belief or conviction is *pistis*. Plato holds *pistis* to be the state of mind induced by persuasion.[75] Aristotle repeatedly uses the term to mean *conviction*.

Such arguments then carry some degree of *conviction* . . .[76]

. . . such are the opinions and propositions that are useful to produce *conviction* in these circumstances . . . But since the object of Rhetoric is judgement . . . it is not only necessary to consider how to make the speech itself demonstrative and *convincing* . . . For it makes a great difference with regard to producing *conviction* . . .[77]

---

[70] *Ibid.*, 1403a, 32.

[71] *Ibid.*, 1381b, 21.

[72] *Ibid.*, 1384a, 23.

[73] Plato, *Theaetetus*, H. N. Fowler, trans. (London, 1921), 201b.

[74] Plato, *Timaeus*, 51 DE.

[75] Plato, *Republic*, 6.509ff.

[76] Aristotle, *Nicomachean Ethics*, H. Rackham, trans. (London, 1926), 1179a, 17.

[77] Aristotle, *Rhetoric*, 1377a, 10ff.

. . . all attendant circumstances, such as noble birth and education, merely conduce to *persuasion* . . .[78]

. . . *we are* most strongly *convinced* when we suppose anything to have been demonstrated . . .[79]

We must refer to what has been demonstrated by the science of optics as our *ground for believing* that our vision is reflected from the air and other substances . . .[80]

This would plead, on the principle of analogy that runs through nature, for the *belief* that it is so in all other cases.[81]

For to all these contentions there is the one *convincing reply* that we can see some things now in motion and now at rest.[82]

In the light of these passages we can see that Aristotle had available to him and was acquainted with two terms, *doxa* and *pistis*, which he could have employed in describing the end, aim, culmination, result, or final cause of rhetoric. But Aristotle eschewed these two terms and, instead, wrote that the object and end of rhetorical discourse was something that is evidently accurately rendered by the English term *judgment*. Whatever else rhetoric meant to Aristotle, it was a faculty that realized its end in the act of judgment. So, at least, we are led to conclude from our examination of Aristotle's own usage of three Greek words.

In considering the scope of Aristotle's theory of rhetoric, we are brought now to conclude that no matter what combination we make of the usages of *krisis* or judgment, or what reasonable extension we are able to make of them, there will remain instances of what we today would call rhetorical persuasion whose objectives, whose accomplishments, whose ends are nothing

---

[78] *Ibid.*, 1367b, 29.

[79] *Ibid.*, 1355a, 5.

[80] Aristotle, *Meteorologica*, H. D. P. Lee, trans. (London, 1952), 372a, 32.

[81] Aristotle, *Physics*, Philip H. Wicksteed and Francis M. Cornford, trans. (London, 1929), 261b, 25.

[82] *Ibid.*, 254a, 35.

that can be called judgment. It suffices to cite the rodomontades of Mussolini, with all their attendant theatrics, or even, at an earlier time, the preaching of John Wesley, to see that there are rhetorical procedures that, far from finding their end in judgment, rather inculcate new convictions by obliterating an audience's capacity for making judgments.[83] As Newman has written,

> The heart is commonly reached, not by the reason, but through the imagination, by means of direct impressions, by the testimony of facts and events, by history, by description. Persons influence us, voices melt us, looks subdue us, deeds inflame us. Many a man will live and die upon a dogma: no man will be a martyr for a conclusion. A conclusion is but an opinion; it is not a thing which *is*, but which we are '*quite sure about*'; and without implying that we doubt. To say that a thing *must* be, is to admit that it *may not be*. No one, I say, will die for his own calculations: he dies for realities.[84]

Substitute "judgment" for "conclusion," and the quotation will serve as a commentary on the *Rhetoric*. Such a substitution would not do violence to the terms, since a judgment is a kind of conclusion, drawn on the merits of competing claims.

It would be impossible to maintain that a judgment is so purely an act of reason as to be unaffected by emotions. We often use such phrases as *biased judgment, prejudiced judgment, unfair judgment,* to refer to judgments we recognize as having gone awry, either through the illegitimate operation of emotions, or because of predispositions that have infected the adjudicatory act. The very fact that we have such phrases is crucial here, for they all imply the existence of some standards of what a judgment ought to be. It is precisely at this point that Aristotle's pronouncements on the end or object of rhetoric illuminate the scope of his theory.

---

[83] Cf. William Sargant, *Battle for the Mind* (New York, 1957), who argues that such discourses as those cited are forms of brainwashing that can best be explained in terms of Pavlovian conditioning.

[84] John Henry Newman, *An Essay in Aid of a Grammar of Assent* (New York, 1898), pp. 70–71.

We apply standards to judgments in such statements as *He rendered a fair judgment* or *His judgment is not good*. We do not apply these same standards, however, to convictions or beliefs. *His belief is good* is not a clear statement. *His coming to hold a belief is good* is a comment on the state of believing rather than on what is believed. We call beliefs or convictions rational or irrational, intelligent or stupid, justified or unjustified, but we do not call them good or bad, as we do judgments. Our standards for evaluating judgments differ patently from our standards for evaluating convictions or beliefs, so that judgment and belief are not synonymous terms. And a rhetorical theory worked out on the assumption that the end of rhetoric is judgment would differ from one that assumed that the end of rhetoric was belief.

The most crucial difference between judgment and belief is that a judgment is supposed to follow from a definitively systematized procedure of adjudication, but the procedures for acquiring or coming to hold beliefs vary so considerably, according to the subject of the belief, that the same procedural standards are not applied. Involved in a judgment is a weighing of claims that are in conflict, and a demand for fair consideration of all sides to a dispute. On the other hand, there is no particular procedure that can or should or cannot or should not lead to a belief. A certain man's conviction that war is an evil may be an inference drawn from evidence; by contrast, his conviction that it is wrong to murder may have been held by him long before he knew of arguments in favor of the belief, and it is highly improbable that any of those arguments could make him any more profoundly convinced of the wrongness of murder than he already was. The processes by which these two beliefs came to be held are quite dissimilar, yet both are beliefs. Many other people have the same beliefs, and though the causative history of each belief may be singular, still these would all be called beliefs, and the processes by which they came to be held would not affect an assessment of them. When we encounter a belief being appraised in terms of the process by which it came to be held, we regard the appraisal as *ad hominem*. But if we suppose the case of a judge passing a judgment on any subject—the merit of a poem, the guilt of a criminal defendant, the value of a political policy, the historical importance of a statesman—by tossing a coin, or consulting a horoscope, or examining the entrails of a bird, we can see that, even though the decision rendered may be just in its consequences, may not miscarry justice, the *judgment* would be regarded as bad. While there is a certain procedure that one is supposed to follow in coming to a judgment, there is no particular procedure that one is supposed to follow in coming to hold a conviction.

Unlike *belief* or *conviction*, the term judgment entails a procedural norm in its very usage. We have a similar normative standard in the case of other words as well. In employing the term art, for example, we may call an atrocious painting executed by an incompetent painter bad art. However, if a painting was bad enough, we would stop calling it art altogether, good or bad. Similarly in the case of poetry, we have no difficulty calling Kilmer's *Trees* bad poetry; but a page of nonsensical gibberish would not be called poetry at all. Anything called by the name poetry, like anything called by the name art or judgment, must have met certain standards before the name will be appropriate. We are not always able to define these standards with precision; hence we can sometimes find reasonable men disagreeing over whether, for example, some of the literature of Dadaism is really poetry, or whether the finger painting of a chimpanzee is really art. Such disputes are usually tiresome, but they do serve to indicate the presence of certain laws of decorum in the uses of these words. In the same way, though we may call a judgment good or bad, if a judgment becomes bad enough we stop calling it a judgment.

There is considerable illumination of the decorum of judgment to be had in considering a now old-fashioned sense of the word prejudice. It was a usage of which Edmund Burke was especially fond, and his employment of it is suggestive:

> You see, Sir, that in this enlightened age I am bold enough
> to confess, that we are generally men of untaught feelings;
> that instead of casting away all our old prejudices, we

cherish them to a very considerable degree, and, to take more shame to ourselves, we cherish them because they are prejudices; and the longer they have lasted, and the more generally they have prevailed, the more we cherish them. We are afraid to put men to live and trade each on his own private stock of reason; because we suspect that this stock in each man is small, and that the individuals would do better to avail themselves of the general bank and capital of nations and of ages. Many of our men of speculation, instead of exploding general prejudices, employ their sagacity to discover the latent wisdom which prevails in them. If they find what they seek, and they seldom fail, they think it more wise to continue the prejudice, with the reason involved, than to cast away the coat of prejudice, and to leave nothing but naked reason; because prejudice, with its reason, has a motive to give action to that reason, and an affection which will give it permanence. Prejudice is of ready application in the emergency; it previously engages the mind in a steady course of wisdom and virtue, and does not leave the man hesitating in the moment of decision, sceptical, puzzled, and unresolved. Prejudice renders a man's virtue his habit; and not a series of unconnected acts. Through just prejudice, his duty becomes a part of his nature.[85]

This use of the term prejudice is especially interesting because of the derivation of the word. It is from the Latin *praejudicium;* literally, before-judgment. It is a predilection, belief, or conviction formed prior to the judgmental process. The term implies the process, and moreover, it implies that the process of judging is a procedure that must meet certain standards, for to call a judgment prejudiced is to condemn it. So, though there is a certain procedure one is supposed to follow in coming to a judgment, there is no particular procedure one is supposed to follow in coming to hold a conviction.

We must be careful to distinguish between the process of coming to hold a belief and the way in which the belief would

---

[85] Edmund Burke, "Reflections on the Revolution in France," *Works* (London, 1894), vol. II, p. 359.

be justified. A belief can be justified quite apart from the procedure followed in coming to hold it; but it seems to be a requirement in the justification of a judgment that the right procedure was followed in forming it. It follows that insofar as Aristotle composed the *Rhetoric* with the judgmental process in view, the scope of his theory would be limited to those forms of discourse that bear some relation to the judgmental process, and rhetorical discourse that finds its end in any state of mind or mental act different from judgment would be excluded from consideration in the *Rhetoric*. This possible limitation on the scope of the *Rhetoric* serves to alert us to the possibility of a corresponding limitation on the scope of neo-Aristotelian criticism.

Parrish has observed that ". . . the judge or listener as Aristotle conceives him is always a *qualified* judge—a person of good education, sound sense, and judicious temper." [86] Given Aristotle's conception of rhetoric as operating to affect the process of judging, and given further the fact that this very process must meet certain normative requirements before it can be considered a judgment at all, it would follow that Aristotle's conception of an audience would be one that met the normative requirements of judges. And when Parrish goes on to recommend to contemporary critics that "this is the kind of audience we must assume in assessing the effectiveness of a speech," [87] he is accepting for neo-Aristotelian criticism the same limitation of scope that Aristotle himself imposed on the province of rhetoric.

The audience that is to be assumed by the neo-Aristotelian critic is not necessarily one of superior insight, sensitivity, or rationality, but only one that adheres to the proprieties of the judgmental process. We must not be misled by the piety with which this assumed audience has been described: there is no divine ordinance holding that the posture of judge necessarily

---

[86] Wayland Maxfield Parrish, "The Study of Speeches," *American Speeches,* ed. Wayland Maxfield Parrish and Marie K. Hochmuth (New York, 1954), p. 12. Parrish's italics.
[87] *Ibid.*

makes one more receptive to truth, or more worthy of it. "Sound sense, and judicious temper" were not the most important characteristics in the audiences assumed by Demosthenes, or Augustine, or Samuel Adams, or William Lloyd Garrison. Moral passion and a capacity for unvarying purposefulness were more important to these rhetors than judicious temper, and are often incompatible with judicious temper. To find the rhetorical discourses of these men and their like wanting because they were not addressed to judges would be to take no account of the audiences to whom they were, in fact, addressed. It would be vain for the critic to try to understand these discourses in terms of a judicatory audience. Here we come upon perhaps the most severe limitation in the scope of Aristotelian rhetoric, a limitation that is most acutely manifested in the Aristotelian doctrine of emotional appeals and in the Aristotelian typology. This limitation consists of a narrow view of human behavior.

To consider first the Aristotelian doctrine of emotional appeals, Aristotle observed that certain patterns of argument will evoke certain emotions in an audience.[88] For example, if a speaker wishes an audience to feel angry, he may attempt to convince them that a barrier is keeping them from a desirable goal, that the barrier is contemptible, unnecessary, unintelligent, or unjust, and that the agent who raised the barrier is disliked by the audience, or considered inferior, or is one whom they had believed above such things. If this pattern of argument is convincingly made, the audience will experience the emotion of anger. In the Aristotelian system, a situation is described and, if the description is accepted as true, the emotion appropriate to that situation follows.

The relationship between the emotion engendered by a discourse and the end attained by that same discourse is circumscribed in Aristotelianism. This relationship is made clear in the following passages.

---

[88] The most comprehensive discussion of emotional appeals in the *Rhetoric* is in bk. ii, ch. 2–11.

Now, previous compilers of "Arts" of Rhetoric have provided us with only a small portion of this art, for proofs are the only things in it that come within the province of art; everything else is merely an accessory. And yet they say nothing about enthymemes which are the body of proof, but chiefly devote their attention to matters outside the subject; for the arousing of prejudice, compassion, anger, and similar emotions has no connexion with the matter in hand, but is directed only to the dicast . . . For it is wrong to warp the dicast's feelings, to arouse him to anger, jealousy, or compassion, which would be like making the rule crooked which one intended to use. Further, it is evident that the only business of the litigant is to prove that the fact in question is or is not so, that it has happened or not; whether it is important or unimportant, just or unjust, in all cases in which the legislator has not laid down a ruling, is a matter for the dicast himself to decide; it is not the business of the litigants to instruct him.[89]

The emotions are all those affections which cause men to change their opinion in regard to their judgements and are accompanied by pleasure and pain; such are anger, pity, fear, and all similar emotions and their contraries.[90]

It is clear from these passages that Aristotle regarded the function of emotional appeals as bending the judgment of the auditor toward a certain bias, "making the rule crooked which one intended to use." Implicit in the conception is a view of rhetorical discourse working to affect the process of judgment. The same conception of the function of emotional appeals appears in other passages.

But since the object of Rhetoric is judgement . . . it is not only necessary to consider how to make the speech itself demonstrative and convincing, but also that the speaker should show himself to be of a certain character and should know how to put the judge into a certain frame of mind . . . for opinions vary, according as men love or

---

[89] Aristotle, *Rhetoric*, 1354a.
[90] *Ibid.*, 1378a.

hate, are wrathful or mild, and things appear either altogether different, or different in degree; for when a man is
favourably disposed towards one on whom he is passing
judgement, he either thinks that the accused has committed no wrong at all or that his offence is trifling; but if
he hates him, the reverse is the case. And if a man desires
anything and has good hopes of getting it, if what is to
come is pleasant, he thinks that it is sure to come to pass
and will be good; but if a man is unemotional or not hope-
ful it is quite the reverse.[91]

The passage clearly discloses the point of view of a man who is
thinking of the judiciary auditor struggling for impartiality and
a firm grip on the truth about the issues before him. This
auditor is a reasonable man, a judge. But what of the auditor
who is uninhibited by judiciary scruples, who gives his prejudices free reign, or who, instead of undertaking the conscious
weighing of claims and counterclaims with the burden of decision consciously upon him, brings to the rhetorical transaction
a *tabula rasa?* The passages do not apply to him. He is outside
the scope of Aristotle's treatment of emotional appeals.

Another peculiarity of the Aristotelian view of emotional
appeals is that it assumes some degree of persuasion to have
occurred prior to the evocation of emotion, and makes the
evocation contingent on the prior persuasion. In this view,
one must believe that a certain situation is true before one will
experience an emotional response. There is even some reason for
believing that Aristotle considered an emotion to be the result
of a judgment, and impossible without a judgment having been
made. Else, in his exegesis of the *Poetics*, finds this view even in
Aristotle's treatment of tragic catharsis.

First of all, so far as the plot as a whole is concerned, if it
is to gain his [the spectator's] sympathy and ultimately his
fear and/or pity, he must make two judgments (one or the
other, and, for the best effect, both): (1) that the hero is

---

[91] *Ibid.*, bk. ii, ch. 1.

"like himself," and (2) that he does not deserve his misfortune. These judgments are not after-effects of the spectator's feeling, they are the prerequisite to it, the conditions which must be satisfied *before his psyche* (that is, the rational element in his soul) *will allow the emotions to be felt.*[92]

It is significant that Aristotle did not think of emotional appeals as carrying arguments or as being means by which ideas are made to become convictions. The *Rhetoric* makes the effectuation of emotional appeals dependent on the audience's having been induced to form a preliminary judgment. The Aristotelian view does not allow for emotional appeals ever to be a primary force in the persuasive process. This type of appeal is always derivative in that its existence is contingent on judgments having been made as a result of other means of persuasion.

Ethos, as a persuasive force, is in the same status as emotional appeals in the Aristotelian treatment; that is, appeals from the character of the persuader are regarded as dependent on other appeals that will make them credible.[93] In the *Rhetoric* only logical appeals are regarded as primary, which is to say that they are rhetorically self-sufficient and do not require extralogical supports for their credibility. The other two types of appeal—emotional and personal—while considered potent means of persuasion by Aristotle, are still derivative, and turn on logical support for their force. This hierarchical view of the means of persuasion is a consequence of the Aristotelian conception of an adjudicatory audience. Judging is a rational process. We speak of emotions or of personal attractions and repulsions as affecting judgment, but never of their producing judgment. It is evident from the immediately preceding quotations from the *Rhetoric* that Aristotle thought of the relationship between judging and the emotions of the judge in the same way. Emotionality is generally considered inimical to the rendering of

---

[92] Gerald F. Else, *Aristotle's Poetics: The Argument* (Cambridge, Mass., 1957), p. 436. Else's italics.
[93] Aristotle, *Rhetoric*, bk. i, ch. 2 and 9; bk. ii, ch. 1; bk. iii, ch. 17.

judgments. We can understand, then, why Aristotle would not regard emotional or personal suasion as central to the function of the audience that is to render a judgment, why he regarded them as "making the rule crooked which one intended to use." These means of persuasion had to be considered ancillary to the presentation of arguments that had direct bearing on the judgment to be rendered.

We are now able to determine that there is at least one important genre of rhetorical discourse that lies outside the purview of Aristotle's theory of rhetoric. That genre is one in which the evocation of an emotional experience in the audience induces belief in the situation to which the emotion is appropriate instead of following as a consequence of belief in the situation. Consider the following passage from Edwards' *Sinners in the Hands of an Angry God:*

> The God that holds you over the pit of hell, much as one holds a spider, or some loathsome insect over the fire, abhors you, and is dreadfully provoked: his wrath towards you burns like fire; he looks upon you as worthy of nothing else, but to be cast into the fire; he is of purer eyes than to bear to have you in his sight; you are ten thousand times more abominable in his eyes, than the most hateful venomous serpent is in ours. You have offended him infinitely more than ever a stubborn rebel did his prince; and yet it is nothing but his hand that holds you from falling into the fire every moment. It is to be ascribed to nothing else, that you did not go to hell the last night; that you was suffered to awake again in this world, after you closed your eyes to sleep. And there is no other reason to be given why you have not dropped into hell since you arose in the morning, but that God's hand has held you up. There is no other reason to be given why you have not gone to hell, since you have sat here in the house of God, provoking his pure eyes by your sinful wicked manner of attending his solemn worship. Yea, there is nothing else that is to be given as a reason why you do not this very moment drop down into hell.
>
> O sinner! Consider the fearful danger you are in: it is a great furnace of wrath, a wide and bottomless pit, full of

the fire of wrath, that you are held over in the hand of that
God, whose wrath is provoked and incensed as much
against you, as against many of the damned in hell. You
hang by a slender thread, with the flames of divine wrath
flashing about it, and ready every moment to singe it, and
burn it asunder; and you have no interest in any Mediator,
and nothing to lay hold of to save yourself, nothing to keep
off the flames of wrath, nothing of your own, nothing that
you ever have done, nothing that you can do, to induce
God to spare you one moment.[94]

Consider now a neo-Aristotelian critic's account of this passage:

> In appealing to fear, Edwards frequently refers to hell. It is
> a very real hell that he pictures, a hell of endless burning of
> the flesh. He is not content with merely describing the
> nature of hell and eternal punishment. He drives home the
> horrors of the torment in each of his listeners. He paints a
> fearful picture and then sets the audience squarely in the
> middle of it. It is a positive, powerful suggestion.[95]

It is easy to detect in the critical commentary something that
inhibits the critic, something that prevents him from really
coming to grips with the discourse. The critic's insight hits the
mark: "He paints a fearful picture and then sets the audience
squarely in the middle of it." Yes, that is exactly what Edwards
does, but it is suggestive that the critic hits the mark only a
glancing blow. He does not go on to an explication of the
rhetorical techniques that make the picture fearful.

In order to account for the passage and fully redeem his sense
of it, the critic would have to turn his attention from its patterns
of argument, which is the usual preoccupation of neo-Aristotelianism, to the texture of its style. He would have to note the
fire imagery running through the passage and relate this imagery

---

[94] Jonathan Edwards, "Sinners in the Hands of an Angry God," *American
Speeches*, ed. Wayland Maxfield Parrish and Marie K. Hochmuth (New
York, 1954), pp. 82–83.

[95] Orville A. Hitchcock, "Jonathan Edwards" in *A History and Criticism of
American Public Address*, vol. I, by William Norwood Brigance (ed.).
Copyright 1960. McGraw-Hill Book Company. Used by permission.

to the *symbolic* force that fire had for Edwards' audience and, to a different extent, for virtually all Western audiences for many centuries. He may even find in the extraordinarily high proportion of monosyllabic words in the passage (187 mono-syllables out of a total of 375 words—almost exactly half!) another key to its power. But the critic's attention does not go in these directions.

We cannot know exactly why this critic has approached the passage in the way that he has. There is no way of establishing that the influence of Aristotle's doctrine of emotional appeals has shaped his critique; but it is at least suggestive that the critique employs the cumbrous and unidiomatic phrase "appeal-ing to fear," with its suggestion that an emotion is something to appeal to and that it will be the result of an argument, and the fact that the critic eschews a systematic investigation of style despite his insight's having led him to the threshold of such an investigation. Perhaps it is this particular critic's temperament that has shaped his critique, or some arbitrary requirements of his study, or some set of reasons we can never know; but it at least invites suspicion that *if* this neo-Aristotelian critic was approaching Edwards' sermons thoroughly under the influence of Aristotle's *Rhetoric*, Aristotle's doctrine of emotional appeals could have led him in the direction he took.

We can find other neo-Aristotelian critics who feel obliged to comment on emotional appeals, but who are evidently laboring under some set of presuppositions that prevent their making incisive commentary. Here is a section entitled "Pathetic and Ethical Proofs" in a critique of the speaking of Theodore Parker:

> In accomplishing proof through the pathetic mode, Parker appealed often to New England's historical pride, particularly in his speeches upon the issue of slavery. The natural concomitant of such appeals was his frequent attack upon proponents of slavery and upon the South as the embodiment of the evil. The element of fear, so preva-lent in early Puritan preaching, Parker did not use; neither

did he appeal to the economic well-being of the individual. Justice and love of fellow men he kept in the foreground as general positive aims; but as pathetic modes he employed the embodiment of their opposites. Although the present reading of Parker's speeches gives little indication of his use of humor, the testimony is that his audiences were visibly amused by his flashes of wit. . . . Parker was conscious of the audience factor in determining the desirable proportion of emotional elements, but the instructional nature of his talk and the power of his thought combined to relegate the strictly pathetic burden, with the exception of his constant attack upon every representation of evil, preponderantly to *Style*.[96]

The critic's subsequent remarks on Parker's style fail to illuminate the emotional force of his speeches, but it is interesting to note how the critic's mind has worked in the paragraphs cited. In an orthodox neo-Aristotelian manner, he has felt obliged to include in his critique a section on emotional appeals, or as he has called it, "pathetic proofs." He senses and notes various motives that Parker attempted to exploit in his speeches, but finally he must "relegate" these motives to the canon of style. Why this curious way of writing? Why this relegation? Does the critic relegate because he expected to account for Parker's emotional tone through Parker's patterns of argument, but then found this impossible? If so, whence the expectation? Again, we can do little more than ask the questions; we cannot read the critic's mind. But when we begin finding this same tendency in one neo-Aristotelian critic after another, we are at least entitled to the suspicion that we have identified not merely a coincidence of idiosyncrasies, but a common cause operating on all these critics: a view of emotional appeals that leads them to expect affective responses to result from arguments, and then distorts their language when their expectation is disappointed. Wallace has a section entitled "Address to the Emotions" in

96 Roy C. McCall, "Theodore Parker" in *A History and Criticism of American Public Address*, vol. I, by William Norwood Brigance (ed.). Copyright 1960. McGraw-Hill Book Company. Used by permission.

his neo-Aristotelian essay on the speaking of Booker T. Washington.

> Beyond skillful selection and amplification of lines of argument that harmonize with the temper and attitudes of his general audience and special groups, Washington stirs up his auditors emotionally. The lines of amplification already set forth, of course, are heavily charged with emotion; they are often concerned with the profit motive, self-interest, duty and responsibility, sympathy and pity. Independent of such emotional address, however, Washington makes a direct attack on the elemental individual by appeals to loyalty, gratitude, fear, pride, and christianity.
>
> But of all emotional means that Washington employs of bringing the hearer and his program together, perhaps the most characteristic is humor.[97]

The remainder of the section on "Address to the Emotions" is devoted to a consideration of Washington's humor. Here again we seem to have a critique influenced by Aristotle's doctrine of emotional proof. The critic looks to appeals to account for the force of the discourses. These appeals are *to* things, to a strange combination: loyalty, gratitude, fear, pride—all emotions, perhaps (though one might swallow some doubt that loyalty is the name of an emotion). But is "christianity" an emotion? Or humor? Is the critic here really looking at the speeches and recording what he sees in idomatic English, or does some system distort his vision or his language or both? In the light of the other neo-Aristotelian essays we have glanced at, we can at least suspect that the difficulties of this critique stem from the very effort to find emotionality appearing as a consequence of arguments, at least in the case of Booker T. Washington's speeches.

In a neo-Aristotelian critique of the rhetorical career of Samuel Gompers the very term emotion is eschewed, and in its place we find a section entitled "Use of Impelling Motives":

---

[97] Karl R. Wallace, "Booker T. Washington" in A *History and Criticism of American Public Address*, Vol. I, by William Norwood Brigance (ed.). Copyright 1960. McGraw-Hill Book Company. Used by permission.

Modern rhetoricians are agreed that human desire is a basic factor in persuasion. Gompers fully recognized the importance of this principle and used it effectively in his speaking. Possessing no dictatorial powers in the Federation, he set about the task of developing a unified labor will through appeals to the impelling motives of the workers.

Soon after the creation of the Federation, Gompers made his first long trip into the Middle West, speaking in thirty-seven cities. In these speeches he assailed revolutionary labor organizations and argued for trade-unionism as the best means of satisfying the workers' wants. . . . He argued for trade-unionism on the grounds that it provided more of the "good things of life"—that is, more pay, shorter hours for labor, more leisure time, more healthful working conditions, etc., the basic wants of laborers everywhere. Radical social reformers might succeed for the moment in getting the attention of the rank and file of labor by talking of ultimate social ends and by arousing a "self-forgetful idealism" among laborers, but they could not compete for long with the astute Gompers, who talked of trade-unionism satisfying the basic wants of self-preservation, private gain, personal power, and pleasure.[98]

We are to believe, then, that prudent self-interest is a more compelling appeal than "self-forgetful idealism," and that this accounts for Gompers' conspicuous success. But was self-interest more compelling to the free laborers who filled the Confederate army during the Civil War? Or to the middle-class leaders of the Bolsheviks during the Russian Revolution? Even the most rigorous of economic determinists acknowledge the existence of "mass opiates," and the attempt of this critic to account for Gompers in terms of an invariably superior appeal is simply not convincing. What the critic discloses is the general pattern of Gompers' arguments; their force remains a mystery. Again, a neo-Aristotelian critic looks to the argument alone to elicit the

---

[98] Walter B. Emery, "Samuel Gompers" in *A History and Criticism of American Public Address*, vol. II, by William Norwood Brigance (ed.). Copyright 1960. McGraw-Hill Book Company. Used by permission.

emotional response in the audience, and does not quite account for that response. And again, the ghost of Aristotle haunts the critical enterprise.

We see how extensively the judicatory conception of audiences has influenced Aristotelian rhetoric and, through it, neo-Aristotelian criticism when we note that the tripartite typology of Aristotelian rhetoric itself is a product of this conception. The deliberative, forensic, and epideictic types are founded on three different objects of judgment or, perhaps more accurately, species of judgment that audiences are supposed to render.[99] If we can find an audience whose response to a rhetorical discourse will not be the rendering of a judgment concerning things past, present, or future, but rather whose response can be described only as a greater or lesser degree of commitment to a conviction, then we will have gone beyond the Aristotelian typology. Aristotelian rhetoric gives us no theoretical foundation for the exegesis of discourses designed for such an audience.

The next chapter will suggest one sort of audience that falls outside the purview of Aristotelian rhetoric, and will suggest a view of rhetorical criticism that may account for such an audience and, more important, for the discourses that create such an audience. Whatever merit that particular account may have— or lack—we can hardly expect the principles of rhetoric formulated two thousand years ago to be uniformly germane today. The nature of political institutions and the modes of communication have drastically changed in twenty centuries. It would be naive to suppose that there would not be concomitant changes in the character of rhetorical discourse, particularly when we know that more subtle modulations in society are echoed in rhetorical discourse.[100] The world changes, and the uses of language with it.

If we contain within ourselves much that the ancient Greeks

---

[99] Aristotle, *Rhetoric*, bk. i, ch. 3; bk. ii, ch. 1.

[100] Cf. Harry Caplan, "The Decay of Eloquence at Rome in the First Century," *Studies in Speech and Drama in Honor of Alexander M. Drummond*, ed. Herbert A. Wichelns (Ithaca, N.Y., 1944), pp. 295–325.

were, we are assuredly more besides, and to add elements to a compound is not to increase it, but to alter its nature. If we "stand astride the shoulders of the ancients," then that necessarily increases our height and modifies our perspective. Thus, to expect ancient principles immutably to apply to mutable phenomena is to place an intolerable burden on those principles. The expectation is unjust to antiquity.

THE ENTHYMEME

There is no better concept with which to illustrate this misplaced antiquarianism than the enthymeme. An impressive number of neo-Aristotelians have insisted on the centrality of the enthymeme in understanding rhetorical discourse, and in this insistence they have done no more than did Aristotle himself. He referred to the enthymeme as "the very body and substance of persuasion." [101] Modern commentators and critics for the last hundred years have reaffirmed this estimate.[102] Moreover, some of these commentators, sometimes wistfully, sometimes indignantly, insist that rhetorical critics of the present time should uniformly place the same high estimate on the enthymeme in the practice of criticism.[103] There can be little doubt that a substantial body of modern neo-Aristotelians regard the enthymeme with the same high respect that Aristotle himself accorded it.

Looked at in broad perspective, the enthymematic system of Aristotle sees persuasion as involving the linguistic management of an audience's common store of values. In the enthymematic

---

[101] Aristotle, *Rhetoric*, Lane Cooper, trans. (New York, 1932), p. 1.

[102] James H. McBurney, "The Place of the Enthymeme in Rhetorical Theory," *Speech Monographs*, III (September 1936), pp. 49–74; Edward H. Madden, "The Enthymeme: Crossroads of Logic, Rhetoric, and Metaphysics," *The Philosophical Review*, LXI (1952), pp. 368–376; Earl W. Wiley, "The Enthymeme: Idiom of Persuasion," *Quarterly Journal of Speech*, XLII (February 1956), pp. 23–24; Charles S. Mudd, "The Enthymeme and Logical Validity," *Quarterly Journal of Speech*, XLV (December 1959), pp. 409–414.

[103] *Ibid.*, McBurney, p. 50; Wiley, pp. 23–24; Mudd, p. 409.

system, an audience is assumed, and this audience is further assumed to share a stockpile of attitudes, of expectations, of scruples and conventions and truisms and commonplaces. The rhetor is conceived of as building his arguments upon various of these common beliefs, employing them as premises that sanction his conclusions.

First, we may ask what application of enthymematic criticism can be made when the common fund of values in a community is disintegrating, and when the auditors of rhetorical discourses are afflicted with moral anarchy and the isolation of the individual from meaningful associations. The enthymematic interpretation of persuasive discourse leads us to infer that persuasion itself is impossible unless there are some cohesive values binding a group together, values on which the persuasive discourse can build its appeals. Yet it is anarchical situations that seem most susceptible to the influence of rhetorical discourse. The accounts of Germany under the Weimar Republic, or of Russia under Nicholas II, disclose situations of extreme and pervasive anxiety on all levels of the society and the rapid deterioration of institutions and ideals that bind people together and supply them with a common fund of attitudes, of cues for feelings, of regulations governing propriety and impropriety.[104] It is at just such moments in history that persuasive discourse asserts its fullest power over human affairs.[105] It is easy to develop a rhetorical system out of commonplace topics if one lives in a walled city, many days' journey from the nearest settlement, with well-established and clearly understood traditions and a culture almost tribal in its cohesiveness, but these conditions hardly

---

[104] R. T. Clark, *The Fall of the German Republic* (London, 1935); V. I. Gurko, *Features and Figures of the Past. Government and Opinion in the Reign of Nicholas II* (Stanford, Calif., 1939), pp. 549–588; Godfrey Scheele, *The Weimar Republic. Overture to the Third Reich* (London, 1945), pp. 145–160.

[105] Leo Lowenthal and Norbert Guterman, "Portrait of the American Agitator," *Public Opinion and Propaganda*, ed. Daniel Katz, Dorwin Cartwright, Samuel Eldersveld, and Alfred McClung Lee (New York, 1954), pp. 474–476.

apply to the political refugee in West Germany or even to the file clerk in Kansas City.

In the face of historical change we can preserve the adequacy of the enthymeme as a true account of persuasion only by extending its meaning. If we posit that the state of moral anarchy and spiritual dispossession that has erupted at periods in modern history, and will erupt again, itself is material for enthymematic premises, then we can redeem the enthymeme as a true and adequate account. But this redemption will have been gained at considerable expense to the precision of the enthymematic system. The major premise of an enthymeme could no longer be considered a value, probability, sign, or example; anxiety is none of these. Rather, it is a term referring to a disquieted state of mind. We can, of course, augment the list of potential enthymematic premises to include states of mind, but in so doing we would render the system of enthymematic analysis less precise, more remote from the world of linguistic action, and less useful, therefore, as a critical instrument.

With these qualifications in mind, we can inquire into the actual usefulness and range of applicability of the enthymematic view of persuasion. We have already noted that the enthymeme assumes a common store of values, beliefs, and commonplaces among auditors, an assumption that is often well founded, but an assumption that is not true at certain critical moments in history. There is, behind the enthymematic system, a second assumption, and one that is far more frequently untrue. That assumption is that men will necessarily accept conclusions if they already believe the premises from which these conclusions have been extracted. In other words, the assumption is that men always behave rationally. We have encountered this assumption before in the present investigation of neo-Aristotelianism. It is an assumption that can be made only of an ideal auditor, in the construction of an ideal rhetoric.

So long as the doctrines of Aristotelianism are applied to rational discourses addressed to judicious audiences, they are useful; but they cannot be extended beyond this scope without misapplication. There is no outrage to reason we can imagine that has not ample historical precedent. In consequence, the assumption of rational behavior that lies behind the enthymeme renders that formulation inapplicable to numberless rhetorical transactions.

In Chapter III we noted the presence of a normative response to a work of fine art and its absence with respect to rhetorical discourses. One can, with effort, imagine what would constitute an ideal audience for Shakespeare, but it simply is not possible to imagine what would constitute an ideal audience for Leon Trotsky. Would it be an audience enraptured by his prose? Then it would not be an ideal audience from the neo-Aristotelian point of view. Would it be a judicious and rational audience with orthodox orientations? Then it would hardly be ideal from Trotsky's point of view. The conception of an ideal audience does not have this kind of application in rhetorical criticism. This being the case, why did Aristotle so manifestly assume an ideal audience in composing the *Rhetoric?*

Evidently, Aristotle was carrying out the program of the *Phaedrus* in a more thorough fashion than his modern disciples appear to suppose. He was contributing to the construction of a normative rhetoric, not a descriptive one. The enthymeme cannot be said to be a characteristic of rhetorical discourse, or even of argumentative discourse, unless one assumes that all audiences will always behave with rational consistency and will, in fact, accept the conclusions that follow of logical necessity from those convictions that they already have. The audience that does not invariably accept the logically necessary implications and entailments of its own beliefs is not the singular aberration. Such audiences are abundantly common. Consequently, it is not descriptively accurate to call the enthymeme "the substance of rhetorical persuasion." [106]

When the propositions in the *Rhetoric* are taken as descriptive statements and applied to rhetorical discourses, some of them always, and most of them sometimes, are palpably in-

---

[106] Aristotle, *Rhetoric*, 1354a, 11. 14–15.

accurate. We are left with one of three possible conclusions: (1) Aristotle was wrong; (2) our manuscript of the *Rhetoric* is hopelessly corrupt; (3) Aristotle was not making descriptive statements.

We should hesitate in drawing the first conclusion on the general principle that Aristotle was likely to have been an observant and reasonable man, to say the least. If we discover an error, then Aristotle was also capable of discovering it and, what is more, of correcting it. In the absence of conclusive evidence to the contrary, the presumption must always be in Aristotle's favor, and that evidence is lacking in the present case.

We are compelled to reject the second conclusion because we simply have no way of knowing how faithful our version of the *Rhetoric* is to the original. The fact that the oldest extant manuscript of the *Rhetoric* dates from the tenth Christian century, about fourteen hundred years after Aristotle's death, invites serious doubts about the fidelity of our version, but at the same time this circumstance makes it possible for us to satisfy these doubts.[107] It is highly improbable—indeed, unthinkable—that extensive corruptions would have left the manuscript internally consistent and also consonant with Aristotle's other extant works, but the *Rhetoric* is both consistent and consonant.

The third possible conclusion is the most feasible: Aristotle was not making statements descriptive of rhetorical transactions. This was not his intention, any more than the *Poetics* is a systematic description of tragedy, or of Greek tragedy, or even of Sophoclean tragedy;[108] any more than the *Organon* is a systematic description of logic, or even of deductive logic.[109]

---

[107] For a discussion of the history of our text see Mederic Dufour, *Aristote Rhétorique* (Paris, 1932), p. 19ff.

[108] Gerald Else, *Aristotle's Poetics: The Argument* (Cambridge, Massachusetts, 1957), p. 446.

[109] Karl Menger, "The New Logic," trans. H. B. Gottlieb and J. K. Senior, *Philosophy of Science*, 4 (July 1937), especially pp. 209–307; Bertrand Russell, *Our Knowledge of the External World as a Field for Scientific Method in Philosophy* (London, 1952), pp. 42–69; Rudolph Carnap, *Introduction to Symbolic Logic and Its Applications*, trans. William H. Meyer and John Wilkinson (New York, 1958), pp. 2–3.

What we have in the *Organon* is a logical system descriptive only of certain kinds of propositional statements; what we have in the *Poetics* is a collection of literary principles descriptive only of a few of the ancient dramas still extant; and what we have in the *Rhetoric* is a system descriptive only of a subspecies of argumentative discourse.

We should not, of course, extravagantly minimize the incomparable contributions of Aristotle to rhetorical theory. The formulation of the enthymeme, for example, remains an extremely useful critical tool for identifying the relationship between some arguments and the auditors to whom they are addressed. However, the persistent efforts of neo-Aristotelian critics to suggest some mysteriously deep importance and elusively rewarding utility for the enthymeme can be regarded more skeptically. What has evidently distracted them is Aristotle's own insistence upon the primacy of the enthymeme as a medium of persuasion. We can understand this insistence not only in view of Aristotle's assumption of a judicious audience, and his reaction against some of the hack rhetoricians of his day, but also in view of the fact that the enthymeme, as we understand it, was an original discovery of Aristotle's.[110] When one gives a new formulation to the world, one interprets this discovery by indicating its importance to thought and the range of its application. This is what Aristotle appears to have done in characterizing the enthymeme as the substance of persuasion. Once the new formulation is absorbed into the main stream of thought, however, claims respecting its importance can be quite misleading. Past a certain point, we no longer need to be reminded of the importance of a formulation. We take it for granted, and pass on beyond it. Perhaps that is why neo-Aristotelians, though they bewail the practicing critic's disregard for the enthymeme, ignore it themselves when they sit down to write criticism.

---

[110] McBurney, "The Place of the Enthymeme in Rhetorical Theory," *Speech Monographs*, III (September 1936), p. 50, n. 3.

It should be clear by now that neo-Aristotelianism is founded upon a restricted view of human behavior, that there are discourses which function in ways not dreamed of in Aristotle's *Rhetoric*, and that there are discourses not designed for rational judges, but for men as they are. It is the task of criticism not to measure these discourses dogmatically against some parochial standard of rationality but, allowing for the immeasurably wide range of human experience, to see them as they really are.

CHAPTER V

An Alternative

Frame of Reference

THE RELATIONSHIP between rhetorical theory and rhetorical criticism is complex and fluctuant, but it is also certain. One cannot compose a theory that anyone will recognize as rhetorical without at least implying certain interpretations and judgments of rhetorical discourses, and one cannot compose rhetorical criticism without assuming, consciously or unconsciously, some theoretical frame of reference. Our task of the moment is to sketch an approach to rhetorical criticism that constitutes an alternative to neo-Aristotelianism, but we cannot approach criticism in a theoretical vacuum. There are assumptions behind any approach, and these assumptions ought to be disclosed as candidly as possible.

Let us imagine a scale whereon rhetorical discourses are arranged according to the intensity of conviction each promoted in audiences. We would find, at one end of the scale, a form of didacticism promoting a disinterested, transitory, tentative approbation. At the other end of the scale we would find a form of suasion promoting radical, permanent, extensive alterations in belief. Between these two extremes, we would find every other sort of rhetorical discourse, distributed according to its latent power to affect human beings. In employing this scale there are certain assumptions we must make.

First, we must assume that there is a limited number of situations in which a rhetor can find himself. *Situation* here refers to the prevailing state of the audience's convictions, the reputation of the rhetor, the popularity and urgency of his subject; in sum, to all the extralinguistic factors that influence an audience's reactions to a rhetorical discourse. To be sure, there may be accidental factors peculiar to a given situation; but our assumption is that there will be a limited number of ways in which rhetorical situations can be characterized, and that the recurrent characteristics of rhetorical situations will make it possible for us—if we know enough—to construct an accurate and exhaustive typology of rhetorical situations.

Second, we must assume that there is a limited number of ways in which a rhetor can and will respond rhetorically to any given situational type. Again, there may be accidents of a given response that will prove to be singular, but on the whole—we assume—there will be only a finite number of rhetorical strategies available to a rhetor in any given situation, and his playing his own variations on these strategies will not prevent the critic from identifying the strategies as characteristic of the situation.

Third, we must assume that the recurrence of a given situational type through history will provide the critic with information on the rhetorical responses available in that situation, and with this information the critic can better understand and evaluate any specific rhetorical discourse in which he may be interested.

Fourth, we must assume that, although we can expect congregations of rhetorical discourses to form at distinct points along the scale, these points will be more or less arbitrary. We can expect such congregations to form because discourses sharing the same characteristics will tend to have the same effects on similar audiences. The postulate we advanced in Chapter II compels this inference. Furthermore, we can expect these points of congregation along the scale to be more or less arbitrary because the important function of a scale is not so much to distinguish entities from one another as to indicate their relations to one another.

We now have three factors that coincide in their behavior: rhetorical strategies, rhetorical situations, and audience effects. If, in a given case, one of these factors is varied, there will likely be concomitant variations in the other two. Now, when we find three factors—strategies, situations, and effects—coinciding, this is a tolerably good reason for suspecting that these three factors we have distinguished are really just three aspects of the same thing. Rhetorical strategies refer to characteristics of the discourse; rhetorical situations refer to extralinguistic influences on the audience; audience effects refer to responses to the strategies in the situations. The fact that these three factors interact suggests that they are constituents of the same phenomenon. We can call this phenomenon a rhetorical transaction. Inasmuch as the discourses arranged along our scale would bear the close relations to other factors that we have posited, we can conclude that ours is a scale of rhetorical transactions.

Scales, as we have noted, indicate relations. A scale of temperature indicates more or less heat. A butcher's scale indicates more or less weight. What, then, does our scale indicate? What sort of relation among rhetorical transactions does it record? In answering these questions, we must be careful to draw a distinction. Both heat and weight are simples; that is, they do not consist of constituents. Either heat or weight may be regarded as a constituent or property or characteristic of something, but nothing can be regarded as a constituent or property or characteristic of heat or weight. Heat and weight are unanalyzable and irreducible. Rhetorical transactions are not simples, however; they are complexes. They are made up of isolable constituents. Consequently, the relations indicated by a scale of rhetorical transactions will be more complicated than the relations indicated by a thermometer or a butcher's scale.

We have found that a rhetorical transaction is a synthesis of three constituents: situations, strategies, and effects. Each of these constituents has its own qualities. For example, a given rhetorical strategy may work to incite an audience to anger. In saying this, we comprehend two of the three elements; we say something about a strategy, and we say something about its effects. We can think of hundreds of adjectives that may, at one time or another, be appropriate to one or two or all three of the constituents of a rhetorical transaction.

We have also noted that no one of these constituents actually operates independent of the others, that to vary one is almost certainly to produce concomitant variations in the other two. Consequently, for us to talk of the qualities of a single of these constituents is really to refer to the qualities of a rhetorical transaction, because none of these constituents is independent of the transaction. Our scale therefore indicates the character of rhetorical transactions. This character of a rhetorical transaction is the concurrence of the qualities of all the constituents of the transaction.

There is yet one other complication we must note. It is that rhetorical transactions are not things; they are processes. As Whitehead said in a more exalted context, the process is the reality. A critic's analysis of a rhetorical transaction is merely a way of talking about it and understanding it. It is quite difficult to discuss processes in the English language. The language is much better adapted to discussing stable entities. Yet any critical statement concerning a rhetorical transaction, no matter what aura of stability it may have, must be applicable to a process if it is to be a valid statement. So, then, we have these two rules of critical writing: First, even though a statement may be so framed as to appear to be about only one constituent of a rhetorical transaction, the statement must really apply to the character of the whole transaction. Second, even though a statement may be so framed as to appear to be about a stable entity, the statement must, in some way, be applicable to a process if it is to be significant for rhetorical transactions.

One question remains about the scale, and that concerns its principle of gradation. A thermometer is graded from cold to hot, a butcher's scale from light to heavy. What is the principle of gradation in a scale of rhetorical transactions? Because rhetorical transactions are not simple, the answer to this question is difficult.

We can construct a scale by any of the constituents of the rhetorical transaction: strategies, situations, or effects. Since these three elements are intimately related and interact, a scale of one will perforce involve the other two. If one has a scale of strategies, for example, it means that this scale will also relate to situations and effects, whether one wants it to or not. This is because certain strategies find their applications in certain situations, and because certain strategies produce certain effects. So, if we construct a scale by any single one of the three constituents of rhetorical transactions, our scale will still be a scale of transactions.

We have varying amounts of information about each of the three constituents of rhetorical transactions. We know relatively little about strategies; certainly not enough to be able to construct a scale of them yet. Our knowledge of rhetorical situations is somewhat fuller, but it is still scanty. We seem to know most about audience effects, for here we can at least imagine a scale of effects ranging from unpersuasive to extremely persuasive. In audience effects, then, we have the material for a rudimentary scale.

As we accumulate more information about rhetorical transactions, we shall be able to enrich our scale. Though at first our scale will be one of intensity of conviction—that is, audience effects, that will by no means be the only element the scale will indicate. Necessarily, the scale will denote the character of rhetorical transactions because intensity of conviction is only one manifestation of this character. As congregations of discourses along the scale are explicated, in the manner that will be illustrated, and we learn more about strategies, situations, and effects, we should eventually acquire a scale disclosing the character of rhetorical transactions with much greater candor than our present paucity of knowledge will permit. In this general direction, at any rate, may lie the methods of a productive rhetorical criticism.

We must now turn to illustrations of this rather abstruse material. Our purposes in illustrating are both to explore the possibilities of a new approach to rhetorical criticism and to clarify, through the consideration of concrete cases, what these possibilities are. To serve such purposes we shall consider, in the remainder of this chapter, a congregation of discourses that may be found toward the end of our hypothetical scale, the end of greater intensity of conviction. We shall arbitrarily assign the generic name *exhortation* to the congregation of discourses we find there. In the next chapter we shall explore a congregation of discourses somewhere nearer the midpoint in our scale.

Throughout our exploration of these two points on the scale, we shall not assume it necessary to pile up a quantity of empirical evidence to establish a generalization. The logic of criticism is not always a logic of probabilities; the recurrence of a phenomenon does not necessarily strengthen a critical generalization. Criticism's rationality, rather, may sometimes resemble the logic of the chemist. Once the chemist has combined two parts hydrogen to one part oxygen to produce water, his formulary generalization is secure. For the chain of events to have occurred once is sufficient to establish it as a potentiality forever. Similarly, when the critic abstracts a formula from a single phenomenon of discourse, that single occurrence is enough to establish the formula. The frequency with which discursive elements occur can establish a critical formula's importance and utility, but it cannot affect the formula's validity. It is with this assumption, too, that we proceed to our exploration.

EXHORTATIVE DISCOURSE

The preceding chapter suggested that as long as rhetorical criticism is confined to the explication of discourses whose only use of emotionality is to bias the judgment of auditors, neo-Aristotelian criticism should function adequately; but once we recognize a genre of discourse that operates differently, then we are outside the purview of Aristotle's theory. Such a genre of discourse is that in which the evocation of an emotional response in the audience induces belief in the situation to which the emotion is appropriate. In this genre, a strong emotional experience does not follow the acceptance of a belief, or even accompany it; it precedes it. Emotion can be said to produce the belief, instead of the reverse.

The excerpt quoted in Chapter IV from Jonathan Edwards' sermon, "Sinners in the Hands of an Angry God," exemplifies the strategy. The excerpt does not have power because its auditors actively believed in hell; if that were the case, then the passage would not have power to the contemporary who does not believe in hell. Rather, Edwards' auditors were made actively to fear hell because his sermon had power. William Lloyd Garrison provides another example of the pattern:

> Why should this not be an occasion of joy instead of sorrow? Listen to those trumpet tones which come swelling on the winds of the Atlantic, and which shall bring an echo from every harp in heaven! If there is joy in that blissful abode over one sinner that repenteth, how mighty and thrilling must it be over a repentent nation! And Great Britain is that nation. Her people are humbling themselves before God, and before those whom they have so long held in bondage. Their voices are breaking in peals of thunder upon the ear of Parliament, demanding the immediate and utter overthrow of slavery in all the colonies; and in obedience to their will the mandate is about being issued by Parliament which shall sever at a blow the chains of eight hundred thousand slaves.

What heart can conceive, what pen or tongue describe, the happiness which must flow from the consummation of this act? That cruel lash which has torn so many tender bodies and is dripping with innocent blood; that lash which has driven so many human victims, like beasts, to their unrequited toil; that lash whose sounds are heard from the rising of the sun to its decline, mingled with the shrieks of bleeding sufferers; that lash is soon to be cast away, never again to wound the flesh or degrade those who are made in the image of God.

And those fetters of iron which have bound so many in ignominious servitude, and wasted their bodies, and borne them down to an untimely grave, shall be shivered in pieces, as the lightning rends the pine, and the victims of tyranny leap forth, "redeemed, regenerated, and disenthralled by the irresistible genius of universal emancipation." And that darkness, which has for so many generations shrouded the minds of the slaves—making them like the brutes that perish—shall give way to the light of freedom and religion. O, how transforming the change! In contemplating it, my imagination overpowers the serenity of my soul and makes language seem poor and despicable.[1]

Garrison, the passionate Abolitionist, was addressing a Negro audience. He was referring to the abolition of slavery in Britain, and his speech continued in the same vein for several more paragraphs. What we have in the speech is, preeminently, the language of emotionality. We do not find in the passage arguments designed to evoke an emotional response; rather, we have language that may evoke an emotional response, and we can readily imagine the acquisition or strengthening of a belief following upon this response.

More than one observer has remarked the tendency of strongly emotional experiences to produce alterations in belief. James, in discussing religious conversion, wrote:

Emotional occasions, especially violent ones, are extremely potent in precipitating mental rearrangements. The sudden

---

[1] William Lloyd Garrison, "Words of Encouragement to the Oppressed," *Famous American Statesmen and Orators*, ed. Alexander F. McClure (New York, 1902), pp. 107–108.

and explosive ways in which love, jealousy, guilt, fear, remorse, or anger can seize upon one are known to everybody. Hope, happiness, security, resolve, emotions characteristic of conversion, can be equally explosive. And emotions that come in this explosive way seldom leave things as they found them.[2]

Freud alluded to a similar occurrence in writing:

We are not used to feeling strong affects without their having any ideational content, and therefore, if the content is missing, we seize as a substitute upon another content which is in some way or other suitable . . .[3]

Murray has provided relevant experimental data through an experiment in which some children, after having been frightened, were asked to rate photographs of people in terms of benignancy and maliciousness.

It was as if the subjects, experiencing an emotion without adequate stimulus, sought something in the external world to justify it—as if the idea had come to mind: "there must be malicious people about." The result of this was that the photographs appeared to change in the direction of adequacy as stimuli.[4]

Finally, Festinger, in considering the psychology of rumor:

The fact reported by Prasad which puzzled us was that following the earthquake [in India, 1934], the vast majority of the rumors that were widely circulated predicted even worse disasters to come in the very near future. Certainly the belief that horrible disasters were about to occur is not a very pleasant belief, and we may ask why rumors that

[2] William James, *The Varieties of Religious Experience* (New York, 1929), p. 198. James cites a large number of cases of religious conversion to support his conclusions.

[3] Sigmund Freud, *Collected Papers*, trans. Alix and James Strachey (London, 1946), vol. II, p. 324.

[4] Henry A. Murray, Jr., "The Effect of Fear Upon Estimates of the Maliciousness of Other Personalities," *Journal of Social Psychology*, 4 (August 1933), p. 324.

were "anxiety provoking" arose and were so widely accepted. Finally a possible answer to this question occurred to us—an answer that held promise of having general application: perhaps these rumors predicting even worse disasters to come were not "anxiety provoking" at all but were rather "anxiety justifying." That is, as a result of the earthquake these people were already frightened, and the rumors served the function of giving them something to be frightened about. Perhaps these rumors provided people with information that fit with the way they already felt.[5]

All of these quotations indicate the disposition of people to accept, sometimes even to seek, beliefs as a consequence of emotional experiences. What we encounter here is assuredly not the Aristotelian pattern of an appropriate feeling-state following upon the rendering of a judgment, such as a feeling of indignation following a determination that a person is guilty of a heinous crime. Rather, this testimony suggests a different pattern: a pattern such as the belief in the guilt of a person occurring as a result of feeling indignation. This is not to say, of course, that the indignation arises spontaneously or that it is unconnected with any ideational stimuli; modern psychology is firmly wedded to the metaphysical assumption that all behavior is responsive, and we shall function within that assumption. More pertinent is the possibility of an affective experience being fastened to a concept that had nothing to do with evoking the experience initially, and the concept comes to be believed because of its association with the affective experience. When this pattern occurs within the consciousness of an individual, the psychologist regards it as a form of rationalization. When we consider the passages from Edwards and Garrison, we find the same pattern being systematically managed through rhetorical discourse. Emotion is used to produce belief.

It will be convenient to refer to the rhetorical discourses relying on this strategy as exhortations, and to define exhortation as

---

[5] Leon Festinger, A Theory of Cognitive Dissonance (Evanston, Ill., 1957), pp. vi–vii. The reference to Prasad is J. A. Prasad, "A Comparative Study of Rumours and Reports in Earthquakes," British Journal of Psychology, 41 (1950), pp. 129–144.

that type of discourse in which the stirring of an audience's emotions is a primary persuasive force rather than—as in Aristotle—a derivative one, and is extensively rather than incidentally used.

The exact means by which audiences are brought to feel strong emotions will, of course, vary from one occasion to the next, depending on the psychological conditions of the auditors, their predispositions, their latent hostilities and affinities, their particular circumstances; but in almost all cases of exhortation certain characteristic strategies will recur.

Since exhortation finds its end in radical conversion, we must place it near the extreme of intense conviction on our hypothetical scale. And, also because of exhortation's power to promote intense conviction, this genre of discourse will, in a sense, be in an alien tongue. It will be alien because its ideas and the values on which they are founded will be initially radical to its uncommitted auditors. The exhorter strives to convey an entirely different way of viewing the world and of reacting, in thought and in feeling, to it. What before was an ordinary convention of behavior to be considered, if at all, with cordial apathy, is now to be an object of intense reprobation. And what before was an extremist notion of a lunatic fringe is now to be an imperative guide to conduct and a cosmic epiphany. The exhorter's immediate problem is one of style.

We are accustomed to receiving new ideas and impressions by a partial adjustment of our views to them and of them to our views. We interpret, and often misinterpret, new experiences by some relatively stable frame of reference that, in its essential characteristics, usually remains unaltered throughout our adult lives.[6] The exhorter means to change the frame of reference from top to bottom. How can he convey his meaning? His is, after all, not an ordinary message, since it would revise the very presuppositions by which ordinary messages are understood. So the

---

[6] For examples of the strength of this frame of reference in shaping new experiences see Eunice Cooper and Marie Jahoda, "The Evasion of Propaganda: How Prejudiced People Respond to Anti-Prejudice Propaganda," *The Journal of Psychology*, 23 (January 1947), pp. 15–25.

first task of exhortation is, ironically, not suasory but didactic: the problem of being understood.

Two attributes of the style of exhortation bear upon the matter of clarity. One of these attributes is the extensive use of concrete description; the other is the frequent substitution of *is* or *will be* for *should* or *should be*. We can find both of these attributes in the passages by Edwards and Garrison quoted earlier.

It is well known that we are much more likely to respond to concrete language than to abstractions, particularly when our convictions are as yet unformed or uncommitted. We would unhesitatingly acknowledge our disapproval of hunger and starvation, but this disapproval would be of a concept merely. We must apprehend specific cases of starvation, either directly, imaginatively, or through the medium of descriptive language, before we experience a strong affective response. Abstract nouns such as democracy, freedom, equality, salvation, the fatherland, power, grace, may, as a result of prior conditioning or prior persuasion, have become so deeply associated with a person's values and point of view that they have the ability to evoke in him an emotional response. But when, at the beginning of a suasive process, one's conversion still hangs in balance, abstractions do not have the power to move one to a new conviction. Some degree of emotional excitation is required in the initial stage, and the language of emotionality is concrete description.

Since radical conversion, which is the end of exhortation, implies the acceptance of a belief as absolutely true, the exhorter commonly bases his appeal on what he claims to be realities. Where the theoretician may conclude that there *ought* to be a revolution, or war, or last judgment, or reform, the exhorter, clad in the mantle of prophecy, proclaims that there *will* be.[7] The exhorter aims, not so much at the inculcation of a belief in the moral superiority of certain modes of behavior, as at a

---

[7] For a discussion of this characteristic's frequent appearance in Nazi, Fascist, and Communist propaganda see Hannah Arendt, *The Origins of Totalitarianism* (New York, 1951), pp. 339–341.

belief that the world *is* a certain way. His concern is only incidentally with the rectitude of his proposals; he is more directly concerned with realities. Therefore his language is characterized by the use of the copula instead of the moral imperative.

Both concrete description and the use of the copula instead of the moral imperative help the exhorter to overcome the initial linguistic impediment between himself and his auditors. The concrete description, more readily grasped than abstractions would be, offers no hindrances to the understanding and, at the same time, serves to stimulate emotionally charged responses. The tone of prophecy gives a greater sense of urgency to the exhortation than would the tone of advising or moralizing. Prophetic utterance avoids the tortuous justifications that moral arguments usually require. Thus the didactic function of the prophetic tone is to simplify discourse.

The auditor of exhortation is subjected to the language of feeling: concrete description. The reasons for his attending at all will vary considerably according to the circumstances of the discourse, the reputation of the exhorter, and the psychological condition of the auditor. Probably the factors that brought the auditor to attend the exhortation in the first place should receive a psychological or sociological account rather than a rhetorical one. In the case of some speeches a contributory cause of attentiveness may be that the auditor beholds a man in a high state of excitement, and listens to him at first in order to discover the reasons for the excitement. It is a primitive response: dilated nostrils, wide eyes, muscular tension, wrinkled brow, heavy breathing, tense voice—all suggest something wrong, and we are alert to discover what, to learn if there is danger to ourselves. We attend. Our remotest ancestors probably had the same response to the same symptoms when language itself consisted of no more than cries of pleasure, pain, or alarm. The description the auditor hears, when given earnest attention, produces emotional reactions such as revulsion, shock, fear, anger, and their like. This emotional reaction, once engendered, and not intensified so rapidly in the exhortation that the auditor's attention is diverted to the techniques being employed on him, finally reaches a point where the auditor must account for his own feelings to himsel.. This self-accounting, urged by the exhorter, involves the acceptance of a conviction. Conversion has occurred.

The reasons for the rhetorical effectiveness of this pattern become quite apparent if we consider what certainly seems to be a universal characteristic of the human condition. The most plausible and reliable source of information we have is our own experience. To become convinced that our experiences have no validity, that the things we see and feel have no justification in fact, would be to undermine our sanity. Only the rare man with singular courage dares to repudiate the reality and value of his immediate experience. Therefore we have a strong proclivity for validating our feelings by accepting appropriate beliefs. The power of exhortation lies, first, in its capacity for evoking intense emotion, and second, in its capacity for legitimatizing the emotional experience with appropriate convictions.[8]

To be terrified by the evangelist's description of the torments to be suffered in hell, and then to believe that there is no hell, is to confess that we have been duped, that a vivid experience of excitement and tension in our personal history is based on a cuckoldry, or a fraud, or a betrayal. Few of us are ever able to make such a self-abasing confession; none of us ever enjoys it. Therefore we are strongly disposed to accept convictions that will justify our having experienced vivid feelings.

The successful use of exhortation by a speaker or writer will enhance his capacity for using it still more on the audience that has first been affected by it. The reasons are similar to those that make exhortation conducive to persuasion at all. Just as the auditor is induced, by the pressure of having to credit his emotional experience, to account for his emotions by accepting a conviction, so too he must credit the agent of his feelings. He

---

[8] Leon Festinger, A *Theory of Cognitive Dissonance* (Evanston, Ill., 1957), propounds the psychological aspects of this view throughout his book. Of course, my vocabulary is not identical with his.

cannot believe simultaneously that the source of his feeling and conviction—the exhorter—is discreditable, and believe in the conviction and experience the feeling too. And once he has granted some credit to the exhorter, he is committed to the easy extension and enhancement of that credit. The result, from the exhorter's point of view, is the strengthening of ethos. Eventually the exhorter may be able to attenuate the process by developing convictions on his word alone, for he has become the agent of truth to his auditors and the validator of their emotions.

One of the many nonrhetorical forces at work in cases of spoken exhortation may be the condition of the auditor as a member of an audience. In such a case, the auditor's private emotions pass into a public domain. He will have accepted beliefs sanctioned by the acceptance of others, and this certainly will sustain him in his new belief. If he is thrown into a group of believers, a certain odium will attach to his skepticism, and this will apply additional pressure on him to believe. If he believes, he not only escapes the odium, he is also rewarded by a relief from the burden of personal responsibility. He need no longer suffer ideological solitude.[9] But this would be, of course, only one of the many nonrhetorical factors at work.

Exhortation may be suggestively compared to the drama in one respect, and the suggestion can serve as a final comment on the basic strategy of exhortation. The auditor of the drama presupposes throughout the play, *If this character were really alive and in this situation, he would act thus and so in fulfilling the conditions of his personality.* For the playwright and the actor to adhere to these conditions, or even to provide unexpected but plausible alternative behavior, is what we call verisimilitude. The auditor of exhortation presupposes, *If I feel this strong emotion, then a certain set of propositions must be true.* The exhorter asserts the antecedent.

[9] See Edith Becker Bennett, "Discussion, Decision, Commitment, and Consensus in 'Group Decision'," *Human Relations*, 8 (no. 3, 1955), pp. 251–273; Kurt Lewin, "Group Decision and Social Change," *Readings in Social Psychology*, ed. Guy E. Swanson, Theodore M. Newcomb, and Eugene L. Hartley (New York, 1952).

SUMMARY

This brief consideration of exhortation has been illustrative only, not exhaustive. We have focussed on a point near the end of our scale of rhetorical discourses—that end of the scale whose ultimate point may be brainwashing or deep hypnosis. Beginning with what we can know best, the audience effect of radical conversion, we have discerned a characteristic strategy that promotes that effect, and we have been able to hypothesize certain qualities of the situation in which this strategy would produce this effect. Thus we have suggested ways in which one sort of rhetorical transaction may be illuminated, and more generally, we have seen how the concept of a scale of rhetorical transactions may be given substance. Incidentally, we have also argued the existence of a genre of rhetorical discourse that, if our interpretation of Aristotle's *Rhetoric* is correct, is outside the scope of neo-Aristotelian criticism. Next we must turn to a fuller explication of another and perhaps more familiar congregation of rhetorical discourses that we would find closer to the midpoint on our scale.

CHAPTER VI

The Genre
of Argumentation

THERE HAS long been recognized to be a congregation of discourses, bearing certain characteristics in common, known as argumentation. The definition of argumentation in a popular textbook can serve as our point of departure in examining the genre.

> Argumentation is probably best defined as the art or activity by which one person, through the use of reasoned discourse, seeks to get other persons to believe or to do what he wants them to believe or to do. Argumentation uses language, discourse. It may be, of course, written language or speech. Whenever either in writing or in speech we seek to get other people to believe or to perform as we want them to,

by the use of language which has a thread of reasoning running through it, we are using argumentation.[1]

It is first worthy of note that this definition, typical of those to be found in textbooks on argumentation, places a stress on reasoning as a distinguishing characteristic of argumentation. Certainly the point is well taken. Argumentation tends to be more carefully reasoned than, say, the Jeremiad, or the call to arms. However, though reasoning is indeed a characteristic of argumentation, it is not a distinctive characteristic. Most discourse is reasoned, in some sense. "Hand over your wallet or I'll shoot you" provides a reason for handing over the wallet, but we are unlikely to consider the statement a sample of argumentation. A reason for believing or doing something may not be reasonable, and the quality that should be emphasized in this preliminary definition of argumentation is not that it is reasoned discourse, but that it is relatively reasonable discourse. This adjective serves better to convey the tone of the genre.

Although the definition quoted above does not make any explicit provision for counterargument to be implicated in argumentation, the implication is accepted by virtually all who use the term, and one can hardly find a systematic treatment of argumentation that does not shade off into considerations of debate, with its suggestion of conflicting points of view. Thus, we may extend our preliminary definition of argumentation: it is not only relatively reasonable discourse, soliciting an assent less intense than, say, exhortation, and more intense than, say, advice-giving, but it is also discourse that occurs in a situation of controversy.

The term *controversy* here must be liberally interpreted. It is not a necessary condition to an argumentative situation that at least two persons, opposed to one another, be present giving utterance to their views. Rather, a person is in an argumentative situation when he addresses himself persuasively to an idea

[1] James H. McBurney, James M. O'Neill, and Glen E. Mills, *Argumentation and Debate: Techniques of a Free Society* (New York, 1951), p. 1.

against which objections are likely to be in his audience's minds. The sources of these objections are likely to be other argumentative discourses. Hence, although a given argumentative discourse may display a formal unity and completeness by itself, it will actually be only a fragment of the process of argumentation impinging on the audience. This compels the rhetorical critic to regard any argumentative discourse with the presumption that it is fragmentary.

The fact the critic of argumentation must take into account is that there are always a protagonist and antagonist in the argumentative situation. The rhetor competes for the assent of his auditors. His case is quite different from that of the poet, who enjoys what Coleridge called ". . . that willing suspension of disbelief for the moment, which constitutes poetic faith." [2] The poet's battle is against a body of entrenched and intransigent prejudices that he must overcome to have an understanding audience.[3] The rhetor has a more active opponent; one who attacks, and who strategically counters the rhetor's own strategies. The poet's task is to overcome the resistance of stale ideas and slothful sensibilities; the rhetor's opposition is kinetic and overtly hostile. The rhetor, then, is compelled to produce discourse that can overcome an active opposition and, simultaneously, contribute to the attractiveness and credibility of the rhetor's ideas. How well or ill the rhetor performs this dual task is an important criterion to the rhetorical critic of argumentation.

To inquire further into argumentation, we must have some samples before us. Let us consider, then, three paradigms of controversy: the Platonic dialogues, the Lincoln-Douglas debates of 1858, and the dispute between Charles Kingsley and John Henry Newman in 1864 that resulted in Newman's composition of the celebrated *Apologia pro Vita sua*. One set of discourses

---

[2] Samuel Taylor Coleridge, *Biographia Literaria*, ed. J. Shawcross (Oxford, England, 1907), vol. II, p. 6.

[3] Cf. I. A. Richards, *Practical Criticism* (London, 1929), especially ch. 5, 7, and 8.

is Greek, one American, and one English. One is ancient and
two are modern. The subjects treated are diverse, ranging from
the nature of rhetoric to the extension of slavery into the American territories to the legitimacy of the claims of the Roman
Catholic Church. Any variables that may affect the inferences
we draw from such evidence seem to be disposed of in the variety
of subjects, issues, and situations represented in these three
bodies of discourse.

STRATEGIES OF ARGUMENTATION

First, the Newman-Kingsley controversy. The religious biography of John Henry Newman is well known: how, as an Anglican minister at Oxford, Newman became one of the leading
controversialists and theologians of the Anglican Church; how
he helped found and was the guiding spirit of the Tractarian
Movement within the Anglican Church; how, in 1845, he dramatically converted to the Roman Church, to the consternation
of his former Anglican colleagues; how, in the eighteen years
following his conversion, he became the forgotten man of English religious discussion, laboring in obscurity as a priest in
Birmingham, regarded with contempt by Anglicans and with
distrust by many Roman Catholics; and how, subsequently, he
attained renown as a Roman Catholic theologian and was ele-
vated to the College of Cardinals.

In 1863, Charles Kingsley, a prominent Anglican Divine,
wrote a review of Froude's *History of England*, Volumes VII
and VIII, for the Christmas issue of *McMillan's Magazine*.
Kingsley chose to make his review the medium of a bitter attack
on the Roman Church, and on all un-English activities in general. Newman's name was not spared in the review, particularly
in a passage that appeared near the middle of the article.

So, again, of the virtue of truth. Truth, for its own sake,
had never been a virtue with the Roman clergy. Father
Newman informs us that it need not, and on the whole

ought not to be; that cunning is the weapon which Heaven has given to the saints wherewith to withstand the brute male force of the wicked world which marries and is given in marriage. Whether his notion be doctrinally correct or not, it is at least historically so.[4]

Kingsley continued his review with a bellicose attack on the Roman clergy. Following the publication of this review, there was some correspondence between Newman and Kingsley, and the February issue of *McMillan's* carried an equivocal apology by Kingsley. Since this apology was not the unequivocal retraction that Newman had expected, a war of pamphlets ensued between the two men bearing on questions of Newman's devotion to truth and that of the Roman Church in general. Between April and June of 1864, Newman brought out a series of pamphlets that ultimately became the *Apologia pro Vita sua*. In a pamphlet entitled *True Mode of Meeting Mr. Kingsley*, which appeared on April 28, 1864—early in the war of pamphlets —Newman announced his rhetorical strategy.

All those separate charges of his had their force in being illustrations of one and the same great imputation. He had a positive idea to illuminate his whole matter, and to stamp it with a form, and to quicken it with an interpretation. He called me a *liar*—a simple, a broad, an intelligible, to the English public a plausible arraignment; but for me, to answer in detail charge one by reason one, and charge two by reason two, and charge three by reason three, and so to proceed through the whole string both of accusations and replies, each of which was to be independent of the rest, this would be certainly labour lost as regards any effective result. What I needed was a corresponding antagonist unity in my defence . . .[5]

---

[4] Charles Kingsley, "Froude's History of England, Vols. VII and VIII," *McMillan's Magazine*, 9 (January 1864), p. 217.

[5] This pamphlet is reprinted in John Henry Cardinal Newman, *Apologia pro Vita sua*, ed. Charles Frederick Harrold (New York, 1947), pp. 385–392. The passage quoted is on p. 389. All further citations from the *Apologia* will be from this edition.

Newman went on to demonstrate that a religious autobiography would serve the need that he had diagnosed, and he followed this pamphlet with the *Apologia*.

The *Apologia* is a record of Newman's struggle to find religious truth, interspersed with frequent quotations from letters he had written in the course of his adult life. Our task now is to discover how the *Apologia* provided Newman with a "corresponding antagonist unity in [his] defence" against Kingsley's imputations of falsehood.

Some note should be taken of Newman's frequent quotations from his own letters.[6] The rhetorical gains Newman realized from this technique served him well in the controversy. The letters tend to establish, first, a consistency of religious concern running throughout his life. It is difficult to regard a man as a calculating liar if you are presented with evidence that his claims and protestations have been earned by a prolonged quest for truth, a quest he reveals in his most intimate correspondence. Second, the letters provided circumstantial evidence that Newman sustained strong and enduring friendships with the recipients of his letters, who were men of high distinction in England. Again the reader is left with the implication that a calculating liar could not perpetuate such relationships over long periods of time without being discovered. The letters, as a literary form and in their tone, serve therefore to repudiate Kingsley's charges. And in their substance, in displaying an earnest and brilliant man moving inexorably, step by step, from Anglicanism to Catholicism, resisting the movement all the while, but compelled to move by the force of his own logic, the letters serve to establish the claims of Roman Catholicism on Newman as rationally irresistible. The letters are at the same time an argument and a defense. They display both the magnetism of Newman's convictions and the ardent veracity of his character. The letters represent a fusion of these disparate tasks in a single rhetorical

---

[6] Walter E. Houghton, *The Art of Newman's Apologia* (New Haven, Conn., 1945), especially pp. 14–16, demonstrates Newman's belief in the value of correspondence as a revelatory biographical medium.

instrument, and the reader who is inclined by the letters to grant one of their implications is moved thereby to grant the other as well. We must note the economy of the strategy, an economy not of style or of evidence, but of influence—an economy that yields the most extensive assent for the least rhetorical investment. By this measure, we can see that once a reader grants a single implication of the letters, he is led to grant all their implications. Once he grants that Newman earnestly sought the truth, then he feels induced to grant that Catholicism is the truth. A congeries of convictions follows in the wake of a single one.

Interestingly, Newman composed a reply to Kingsley in dialogue form early in the controversy.[7] This brief, incisive dialogue shows Newman's mastery of the form. It was a form clearly available to him, in the sense that he understood it and could adapt it to his ends. Why, then, did he abandon the form in composing the *Apologia*, or better, in favor of the *Apologia*? Some critics have suggested a psychological explanation.

The most frequent critical attack on the *Apologia* is that it is egotistical.[8] This accusation would leave us with the conclusion that Newman abandoned the dialogue in favor of autobiographical apologetics so that, in neurotic service to his pride, he could speak in his own voice exclusively. Whatever merit the accusation has as an explanation of Newman's motives, it fails entirely to account for the impact of the discourse on human affairs. The question we may more profitably raise is, Does the apologetical form offer rhetorical advantages over the dialogue?

The first and most obvious answer is that a change from the

---

[7] The dialogue appears as an addendum to the Newman-Kingsley correspondence that Newman published as a pamphlet in February, 1864, under the title, "Mr. Kingsley and Dr. Newman: A Correspondence on the Question Whether Dr. Newman Teaches that Truth is No Virtue." Reprinted in *Apologia*, pp. 371–372.

[8] For a review of these attacks see Charles Frederick Harrold, *John Henry Newman. An Expository and Critical Study of His Mind, Thought and Art* (New York, 1945), pp. 312–313.

dialogue to apologetics purges the discourse of the antagonist and his views. Newman was, of course, the sole creator of his dialogue with Kingsley, as Plato was of his dialogues, and he could, as Plato did, reduce the antagonist to an instrument for progressively revealing, in a favorable light, the views being urged by the author of the dialogue. If the antagonist is only a tool for the progressive and favorable exegesis of the rhetor's own point of view, and if, in his bumbling and equivocation and susceptibility to logical traps, this puppet antagonist tends to undermine the real opponent and to caricature him, why be rid of so useful a device? Why silence the antagonist if his every statement serves the rhetor's ends in such a variety of ways? The questions become even more provocative if we turn from Newman to Plato, for we find in Plato the same progressive tendency to escape the strictures of the dialogue form. Some of the earlier dialogues, like the *Gorgias* and the *Phaedo*, sustain a strict adherence to this form, while in later dialogues, like the *Phaedrus*, the *Symposium*, and the *Laws*, we find an increasing number of long speeches from the protagonist and a decreasing expression of antagonistic views by subsidiary characters. Indeed, in few of the dialogues of Plato's middle and late periods do we find antagonists at all. Rather, we find subsidiary characters overtly cooperating with the protagonist in the exegesis of his doctrine.

Perhaps the answer to our puzzle is suggested by Kenneth Burke's conception of literary "transcendence." [9] What we have in the *Apologia* is not so much a continuation of Newman's controversy with Kingsley as an engulfment of that controversy. The attention of the auditor is turned to ideas that subsume the issues of the original dispute. Newman announced his intention of projecting the controversy onto a new level in the concluding paragraph of his pamphlet of April 21, 1864, *Mr. Kingsley's Method of Disputation*.

---

[9] Kenneth Burke, *A Rhetoric of Motives* (New York, 1950), pp. 10–13, *et passim*.

And now I am in a train of thought higher and more serene
than any which slanders can disturb. Away with you, Mr.
Kingsley, and fly into space. Your name shall occur again
as little as I can help, in the course of these pages. I shall
henceforth occupy myself not with you, but with your
charges.[10]

True to his word, Newman did not enter Kingsley's name into
the text of the *Apologia*.

How are we to describe this new level onto which Newman
brought the controversy? One way may be to say that Newman,
in the *Apologia*, propounded a conceptual synthesis that absorbed both the original thesis and its antithesis. The controversy began with the simple thesis *Newman cares not for truth*.
This thesis is answered not by a direct denial, but by the *Apologia*, which represents Newman, in prayerful anguish, patiently
constructing an intricate hierarchy of values that finally satisfies
his quest for certitude. Confronted with this representation, the
reader is no longer disposed either to assert or to deny that Newman cares not for truth; or, to be precise, the reader is not disposed to deny Kingsley's thesis, and finds it now impossible to
affirm. The question of Newman's veracity is trivial before the
epiphany Newman has drawn forth.

The same strategy occurs in Plato. An antagonist like Gorgias
is directly refuted in the *Gorgias*, but the middle and late dialogues, which construct a new frame of reference for viewing
and valuing things, do not directly refute such a character as
Gorgias; rather, they take no account of him. Again, the discourse is projected onto a new level that leaves the old controversy behind. Or better, the issues of the old controversy are
now seen to be minor elements in a complex system of thought
that comprehends many more issues than are included in the
old controversy.

To counter this strategy the antagonist can no longer merely
amplify his arguments. His task is to overturn a complex system

---

[10] Reprinted in *Apologia*, pp. 384–385.

of thought. The rhetor has abandoned dialogue form, has, in fact, abandoned controversy itself as a form in favor of the elaboration of a synthetic concept much greater in scope than the issues of the original controversy. The rhetor, in taking his auditors with him in the abandonment, wins the controversy either by converting some of his auditors to his synopsis or, in the case of the unconverted auditors, by default, his antagonist having no reply to this new synthesis.

In turning to the Lincoln-Douglas debates of 1858, we find that both participants had the materials for synthesis, though neither succeeded in making one. In the case of Douglas, the embryo of argumentative synthesis lay in his ideal of Popular Sovereignty. Douglas faced a situation in which his constituents were becoming increasingly agitated and divided over the question whether slavery was to be allowed into the territories. His rhetorical challenge was to identify himself with some policy or principle by which he could satisfy this question and at the same time unite the dissident elements in his own state in 1858 and begin developing a platform with national appeal for the presidential election of 1860. Douglas's response to this challenge was Popular Sovereignty—the doctrine that held it to be the business of each state and territory to determine, within its own borders, what status the Negro shall have.

Popular Sovereignty served Douglas's needs in a number of ways. First, it did not, on its surface, alienate any faction in the slavery controversy except the Radical Abolitionists, whose support Douglas knew to be lost to him in any case. Second, Popular Sovereignty enabled Douglas to swing to the offensive and accuse Lincoln and the Republicans of making disruptively sectional appeals. Third, and perhaps most important to our consideration of argumentative synthesis, the doctrine was appealing as a principle, as well as prudentially, since the right of a community to determine its own method of government and its own social system had long been acknowledged an essential element of democratic society. Fourth, the policy was one Douglas had long espoused in his senatorial career, and so was one with which he could achieve a close identification in the minds of the electorate. And fifth, the policy was all but invulnerable from direct attack; the principle of self-determination was such a deeply held conviction that, as a principle, it was not the subject of debate any longer. Such were the multiform advantages Douglas could realize from his advocacy of Popular Sovereignty.

Despite these rhetorical advantages that Popular Sovereignty was capable of yielding Douglas, he was not successful in imposing his point of view on the debates. Popular Sovereignty is argumentatively involved in a complex view of political behavior that constitutes its rationale. This view, if elaborated by Douglas, might have forced Lincoln into an impossible argumentative position either by compelling him to attack the principle of self-determination, or by compelling his silence on the question of extending slavery to the western territories. Lincoln was, in fact, hard pressed in the early debates to reconcile his agreement with the principle of Popular Sovereignty and his opposition to slavery. For reasons that remain mysterious, Douglas did not elaborate the doctrine of Popular Sovereignty much beyond its initial statement, so that the concept, which might have become an argumentative synthesis for Douglas even more compelling than it was, did not realize its potentialities in the debates.

Lincoln's opposition to the extension of slavery, involved as this opposition was in a complex body of moral attitudes, also held the promise of argumentative synthesis, but that promise was not realized in the debates of 1858. Lincoln's position in the debates, at first defensive and slow to crystallize, finally congealed around the principle that slavery was wrong, and as such, could not be indefinitely tolerated. Lincoln deliberately made his campaign rise or fall on this moral judgment, implicating, as he did, this judgment with almost all the other arguments he advanced during the second half of the campaign. His methods of defending this judgment were to establish a relationship between it and the traditions of the country, particularly the ideals embodied in the Declaration of Independence and the intentions expressed by the Founding Fathers, and to reiterate the judgment in vigorous and imaginative language, presumably in the belief that accepting slavery as an evil was mainly a matter of perceiving its nature clearly enough. But again, the synthetic potentialities of the principle were not fulfilled.

It should be said, in critical fidelity to the Lincoln-Douglas debates, that Lincoln made more progress than did Douglas from thesis to synthesis, from attacking and defending specific issues to elaborating a synoptic view that would subsume and subordinate his opponent's position. However, Douglas was closer to synthesis when the debates began. The idea of Popular Sovereignty was already fairly well elaborated in the first debate at Ottawa, but its implications were never well developed by Douglas. Douglas took no pains to relate his principle to correlative ideas in order to achieve an argumentative synthesis. Lincoln, for his part, did not unequivocally propound his opposition to slavery until the fifth debate, at Galesburg, leaving only two more encounters for the elaboration. Consequently, the end of the debates found the issues joined so evenly and securely that the debates themselves were inconclusive. Lincoln narrowly won the plurality of popular votes, but Douglas was returned to the Senate by the Illinois legislature. Neither man's view finally prevailed, and neither man was discredited. Both points of view remained intact for the presidential election of 1860, which, though it was historically fateful, was itself argumentatively inconclusive. The resources of argument failed, in the 1850's, to achieve a national consensus on the question of slavery, and while no one could prove that this perpetuation of controversy caused the Civil War, it seems undeniable that it was a prerequisite to that war.

The foregoing consideration of the Lincoln-Douglas debates has illustrated the application of a critical principle suggested by the Newman-Kingsley controversy and the Platonic dialogues. Two matters are clarified by this application. First, the principle of argumentative synthesis, as applied to all three paradigms, relates to the resolution of controversy. That is to say, the principle does not give us information about the genesis of debate, nor about its texture; it gives us information about its structure.[11] Second, the principle raises a larger question concerning the ends of debate on public issues.

The investigations of argumentative discourses that have been guided by neo-Aristotelian criticism have, on the whole, been preoccupied with the processes of controversy, and have paid little heed to the resolution of controversy.[12] Neo-Aristotelian critics seem to assume that disputes expressed through rhetorical discourses will be resolved by judgments that audiences express in some fashion. But the Lincoln-Douglas debates exemplify a controversy that was never resolved under any system of discourse, a controversy that proceeded finally into civil war.

The simple notion that argumentation finds its end in judgment, or even in the persuasion of an audience, will not account for the cases of argumentation that we actually encounter. Inasmuch as the years of controversy preceding the Civil War failed to avert that war, failed to achieve a national consensus on the issue of slavery, must the critic conclude that no parties to the controversy achieved their ends? How will the critic assess the *Apologia pro Vita sua*, which did not send England into the Church of Rome, but which did vindicate a distinguished career and silence an irresponsible bigot? Even when we confine ourselves to rhetorical considerations only, we are forced to conclude that controversy serves other ends in addition to judgment, or

---

[11] For the distinction between texture and structure see John Crowe Ransom, "Criticism as Pure Speculation," *The Intent of the Critic*, ed. Donald A. Stauffer (Princeton, N.J., 1941).

[12] See, e.g., Marvin G. Bauer, "Persuasive Methods in the Lincoln-Douglas Debates," *Quarterly Journal of Speech*, XIII (February 1927), pp. 29–39; Edward Z. Rowell, "Prolegomena to Argumentation," Part I, *Quarterly Journal of Speech*, XVIII (February 1932), pp. 1–13; Part II, *Quarterly Journal of Speech*, XVIII (April 1932), pp. 224–248; Part III, *Quarterly Journal of Speech*, XVIII (June 1932), pp. 381–405; Gale L. Richards, "A Case Study in Deliberative Persuasion: John Marshall's Congressional Speech on Jonathan Robbins," *Speech Monographs*, XXI (November 1954), pp. 254–266; William R. DeMougeot, "Argumentation in the National Health Insurance Movement, 1932–1940," unpublished dissertation (Cornell University, 1959). A noteworthy exception to my generalization is Leland M. Griffin, "The Rhetorical Structure of the Antimasonic Movement," *The Rhetorical Idiom. Essays in Rhetoric, Oratory, Language, and Drama*, ed. Donald C. Bryant (Ithaca, N.Y., 1958), pp. 145–160. Griffin's essay is neither Aristotelian nor textural.

even to persuasion. Perhaps controversy serves other ends *instead of* judgment or persuasion, at times. Clearly no critical theory can proceed much beyond its most rudimentary formulations without some firm conception of the functions of the activity it is designed to understand and appraise.

THE FUNCTIONS OF ARGUMENTATION

One function of argumentative discourse we must posit is a dissuasive function. Argumentation serves not only to persuade people sometimes to accept convictions, but also to dissuade them from other convictions; that is, argument makes some ideas unacceptable. Argumentative situations are those in which incompatible ideas are brought into open conflict. Occasionally in the course of controversy the disputants discover that ideas that seemed incompatible are not, that differing points of view can be accommodated to one another. But more often thesis and antithesis become rigid and unmalleable, and for one idea to live, the other must die.

There are circumstances in which a society cannot sustain a controversy indefinitely. Athens, lured to compromise with Macedonia by the party of Aeschines, and then attracted to a firm anti-Macedonian position by the party of Demosthenes, vacillated between the conflicting advocates until no real choice was left; the anti-Macedonian alliance urged by Demosthenes was no longer feasible, and the armies of Macedon were at the gates of the city. The failure of the Western parliamentary governments to deal decisively with Hitler's early adventures in Spain, in the Rhineland, and in Czechoslovakia are also examples of dispute continuing past the point of decision, compelling men to forfeit their judgments to events. The clear rejection of an idea will, on occasion, shape an historical epoch. Nowhere so much as in argumentation have we incompatible ideas in conflict with one another, and therefore in no other form of rhetorical discourse does dissuasion appear as so important a characteristic.

There are at least two objects on which dissuasion operates in an argumentative situation. The first of these is the rhetor himself. Argumentation, in committing rhetors to firm and increasingly well-defined positions, works to prohibit to them other positions that, in the course of controversy, become concomitantly firm and well defined. Almost all arguments deny in the act of affirming, and exclude some endorsements in the very process of extending others. Therefore the consideration of any specimen of argumentative discourse can relevantly concern itself with the conceptual avenues closed by the discourse as well as with the sequence of inferences implied by it. When Plato or Newman or Lincoln or Douglas makes an argument, promulgates a doctrine, takes a stand, the effect of the act is not only to oblige him to further discourse of a certain character, but also positively to prohibit to him other discourse of a different character. This is one of the invariable conventions of controversy.

Ordinarily we are most attentive to the positive aspects of doctrinal propositions; that is to say, we are most interested in the convictions a person has acquired and is implicatively committed to when he has pronounced an affirmation upon a controversy. But it is equally necessary in the case of argumentation to regard the negative aspects of doctrinal propositions—that is, the alternative affirmations that are closed to a person once he has chosen one affirmation from among competing and mutually exclusive options.

In considering the dissuasive function of argumentation on rhetors, we find a ready example in Douglas's strategy of identifying himself with Popular Sovereignty. His opening speech in the Galesburg debate contains a passage that, with only minor alterations in phraseology, Douglas reiterated throughout the campaign of 1858.

> I say to you, frankly, that in my opinion this government was made by our fathers on the white basis. It was made by white men for the benefit of white men and their posterity forever, and was intended to be administered by white men in all time to come. But while I hold that under our consti-

tution and political system, the negro [sic] is not a citizen, cannot be a citizen, and ought not to be a citizen, it does not follow by any means that he should be a slave. On the contrary it does follow that the negro, as an inferior race, ought to possess every right, every privilege, every immunity which he can safely exercise consistent with the safety of the society in which he lives. Humanity requires, and Christianity commands that you shall extend to every inferior being, and every dependent being, all the privileges, immunities and advantages which can be granted to them [sic] consistent with the safety of society. If you ask me the nature and extent of these privileges, I answer that that is a question which the people of each state must decide for themselves.[18]

Even a cursory reading of this passage will reveal its reflexively dissuasive character. It is an argument that began by denying the right of the Negro to hold citizenship and ended by affirming the right of Maine, or of New York, or of any state to grant the Negro citizenship. It held out a principle of paternalistic benevolence to the Negro, and took away any meaning that could be attached to this principle by endorsing in advance any interpretation that any state or territory chose to make of it. In sum, Douglas's own exegesis of Popular Sovereignty revealed it to be a principle that committed him to repudiating every general statement made on the morality of slavery and Negro rights, for the principle obliged Douglas to yield the integrity of any moral generalization to the contravention of a single state or territory. Here we have encountered the negative aspects of Douglas's strategy: with Popular Sovereignty, as he interpreted it, Douglas could have taken no national position on the slavery question. As an Illinoisan, Douglas did have it open for him to say, "Slavery is wrong in Illinois." But if he were confronted with the question of the moral status of slavery in Alabama, his lips would have been sealed. He could not say,

18 Paul M. Angle, ed. Created Equal? The Complete Lincoln-Douglas Debates of 1858 (Chicago, 1958), pp. 294–295.

"Slavery is wrong in Alabama," for from that statement it would have been but a short and inevitable step to the statement, "Slavery should not exist in Alabama." This was Abolitionist doctrine. This would have delivered Douglas into the arms of the Republicans. Lincoln, then, knew what he was doing when finally, in the course of the debates, he began emphasizing the turpitude of slavery in general and throwing this proposition into Douglas's face with a dare. And Douglas, too, knew what he was doing in refusing the dare. But note: Douglas's silence on the morality of slavery was not imposed on him by anything but the particular tactic he had adopted. By a series of affirmations he chose to pronounce, another body of affirmations, not even contradictory, but argumentatively incompatible, was closed to him. Not until artillery had fired on Fort Sumter and the country ran with fraternal blood was Douglas released from his own web of argument. Thus did argumentation serve as a reflexive dissuasion, prohibiting to the rhetor certain doctrines that, prior to his arguments, were available to his choice.

The dissuasive function of argumentation on auditors is a better known phenomenon, if not a better understood one. Insofar as one set of ideas gains an ascendency in the minds of auditors, other, incompatible ideas are rejected. Here again, argumentation functions dissuasively. The auditor of a dispute, once his interests have been enlisted, is confronted with a choice. The choice may be real or fictitious in the reality of the situation, but real or not, the auditor feels himself confronted with a choice, and frequently he feels himself impelled by necessity to make a choice. His acceptance of one set of ideas will usually involve his rejection of another. The two acts, distinctive under analysis, are usually so conjoined in the argumentative situation that they occur simultaneously. This characteristic of controversy is familiar. Less well known is the nature of the choice with which the auditor is presented. An inquiry into the nature of the choice brings us to the question, What is argumentative incompatibility?

ARGUMENTATIVE COMPATIBILITY

Incompatibility, as here used, does not mean the same as contradiction. Controversy does not always present contradictory positions. For example, to note only the contradictions that materialized in the conflict between Newman and Kingsley would be to account for only a small proportion of the rhetorical activity in their dispute. Kingsley did not call Newman a liar; he merely left the inference to be drawn. And Newman did not characterize himself as a man devoted to truth; again, he merely left the inference to be drawn. If we were to inspect the discourses of the two men in order to find pairs of contradictory statements, we would find few, and those not especially important. Incompatibility, then, is a term that is rhetorical rather than logical, and it refers to a relationship pertinent to rhetorical criticism rather than to logical analysis.

We can better understand the distinction between incompatibility and contradiction by noting that there are situations in which the terms are mutually exclusive. There are incompatibles that are not contradictions. For an example we have only to recall the concepts of Popular Sovereignty and opposition to the extension of slavery as they were developed during the Illinois senatorial campaign of 1858 and afterward, in legislative debate, up to the Civil War. A logician could find no fault with the statement, "I am in favor of each state's determining its own affairs, and I am opposed to the extension or perpetuation of slavery." This is no contradiction. However, it seemed to a vast number of Americans between 1858 and 1860 that, on the level of practical affairs, there was no way of implementing the policies implicit in this statement. In short, these people would have found the two endorsements in the statement incompatible with one another.

To clarify incompatibility itself, it is first necessary to stipulate some preliminary definitions. In the pages to follow, the term belief will be used to refer to an idea one has an inclination to affirm or accept as true, good, wise, or prudent. The term disbelief will be used to refer to an idea one is inclined to deny or reject as false, evil, unwise, or imprudent. Between belief and disbelief is unbelief, which will refer to a disinclination either to affirm or deny—neutrality, indifference. Belief and disbelief both entail active states of mind; unbelief refers to a passive state of mind. Belief is the consequence of persuasion; disbelief is the consequence of dissuasion. To believe and to disbelieve are the verbal forms referring to the ways in which beliefs and disbeliefs, respectively, are held.

Incompatibility seems to occur at the nexus of a situation in which an audience is confronted with a choice between two or more beliefs, or between two or more disbeliefs. In the first case, the choice confronting the audience will be that of disbelieving one of their beliefs in the act of granting another belief. In the second case, the audience will be confronted with the choice of believing one of their disbeliefs in the act of accepting another disbelief. Whenever rhetorical positions confront one another, each claiming allegiance to a disbelief that requires belief in the other, a situation of argumentative incompatibility has been established.

Argumentative incompatibility simply refers to the mutual exclusivity of beliefs or disbeliefs; but it is an exclusivity founded not upon the law of contradiction, but upon an audience's inclination to affirm or deny. These inclinations in an audience may exist before, during, or after their hearing or reading rhetorical discourses; but argumentative incompatibility occurs when and so long as the audience confronts the choices described above.

The critic may apprise himself of the existence of argumentative incompatibility in any one of several ways. He may have the testimony of reliable auditors that certain choices presented to them in rhetorical discourses were incompatible, but such evidence is rare. More likely the critic will find evidence of incompatibility in the discourse of disputants who so express themselves as to make the incompatibility clear. For example, a reading of the Lincoln-Douglas debates leaves no doubt that Douglas's interpretation of Popular Sovereignty was incompatible with Lincoln's views on slavery—incompatible, that is, to their Illinois audiences. The critic can infer from the texts of the debates that this was the interpretation of the Illinois audience of 1858 made by both Lincoln and Douglas. Since each man was in a position to know his audience well and was especially perceptive in analyzing audiences, the evidence would be strong. Moreover, the very fact that Lincoln and Douglas insistently approached their subjects so as to make their positions incompatible served as a kind of guarantee that their analyses of their audience would be made correct by the debates themselves. Finally, the critic may be able to employ evidence from the discourses of a certain type of rhetor whom we can call the mimetic-orator. The function of the mimetic-orator is not to shape an audience's beliefs and disbeliefs but to reflect them. He is the spokesman, official or unofficial, of some group in society, and his discourses may be taken as expressing the mind of that group. Norman Vincent Peale is a conspicuous example of the mimetic-orator: his discourses reflect and confirm the convictions of a group without altering those convictions to any measurable degree. The discourses of the mimetic-orator, once they have been properly identified, may be a source of information to the critic on whether certain ideas will be incompatible to the audience the mimetic-orator reflects.

It should be apparent that a situation of argumentative incompatibility is such only with respect to a given group of auditors. Therefore, the determination of incompatibility cannot be made solely on an examination of discourse. The interpretation of the discourse in relation to an audience is necessary in determining incompatibility.

Thus far we have considered incompatibility as it appears in the competition for assent between opposing points of view. Incompatibility can also occur within the discourse of a single rhetor. A unitary discourse may express ideas that are incompatible with one another. The source of this incompatibility would, again, be in the effects of the discourse on auditors. A rhetor arguing allegiance to a belief his auditors already hold, but whose arguments entail disbelief in another belief his auditors hold would be presenting incompatible arguments to that audience. Or, a rhetor who, in the course of arguing allegiance to a disbelief his audience already holds, entails allegiance to a belief his audience disbelieves would be presenting incompatible arguments to that audience. An example of the first case would be arguing before the United States Chamber of Commerce that taxes on dividends should be reduced because the resentment caused by the reduction would help bring down the whole system of private investment. An example of the second case would be arguing before the Fellowship of Reconciliation, a pacifist group, that war is evil because too many people escape it with their lives.

CLUSTERS OF OPINION

There are specific beliefs and disbeliefs that, in many people, hang together as constituents of a general point of view. For example, racism, anti-semitism, ultranationalism, religious fundamentalism, and "states-rightsism" form a cluster of opinions held by some of our countrymen. The exhibition of one of these opinions is a fallible sign of the existence of the others. The major political parties of the United States and England provide manifest evidence of this coalescence of convictions: each party represents a body of beliefs and disbeliefs on a wide range of subjects, and each contains a core of subscribers who, in their individual convictions, adhere to the party line with fair consistency. This adherence is not the result of directives from political leaders—though it is undoubtedly influenced by suggestion from leaders—but it makes possible the existence in both countries of a doctrinaire liberalism and a doctrinaire conservatism. (Another way of describing incompatibility is to say that a rhetor, in arguing in support of an opinion whose argumentative procedures bring him or seem to bring him into opposition to another of the opinions belonging to the same cluster, will seem to the audience holding this cluster of opinions to have presented incompatible arguments. Or, given an audience that opposes each member of a cluster of opinions, the rhetor who seems to endorse one opinion of the cluster in opposing another will have provided this audience with incompatible arguments.)

The links among opinions in a cluster are mystifying. They are not the links of logical entailment: few men are so philosophical as to believe by inference alone. In individual cases one can find psychological reasons for a person's holding a certain group of beliefs and disbeliefs, and these psychological reasons may supply the common element in disparate convictions. The explanation for a man's believing in the inferiority of the Negro and in repeal of the income tax may be simply that he acquired these beliefs from his father who, to him, was an immensely authoritative figure. With the paternal explanation, one may be able to account for many of this man's allegiances and for much of his behavior; but if the rhetorical critic wishes to account for the allegiances and behavior of a large group of people, the paternal explanation will be impractical.

A sociological explanation—for example, that a certain group of opinions gained adherents because of the anxieties of the Cold War—would be more useful to the rhetorical critic: it would enable him to comprehend audiences as groups rather than as individuals; but it would have defects too. The sociological explanation will not account for the strength of one cluster of opinions over another cluster; it will not enable us to see audiences in argumentative situations where points of view are competing for their allegiance. The rhetorical critic requires a method of analysis that enables him to connect the convictions that people have with the discourses that they hear and read. This requirement does not negate the merits of psychological or sociological accounts of rhetorical behavior; it is merely incommensurable with those accounts. In the final analysis, the rhetorical critic has to illuminate the character and effects of rhetorical discourse. He is a student of language. As such, he will find it necessary to emphasize different aspects of the rhetorical situation from those emphasized by the psychologist or the sociologist, and he will find it necessary to evolve a vocabulary of his own for accounting for those social and psychological forces that are particularly pertinent to his purpose.

Generally, the psychologist or the sociologist, if he interests himself at all in the convictions of a man or a group, has a broader interest than the rhetorician in the genesis of these convictions, and a narrower interest in the fact of their existence. The psychologist or the sociologist seeks to comprehend entirely the genesis of beliefs and disbeliefs; if this objective takes him into the personal history of an individual or the analysis of a social force, then he follows his leads. The rhetorician, on the other hand, is interested in the single force of rhetorical discourse. In sum, the psychologist and sociologist may be interested in the geneses of all the convictions engendered by or affecting rhetorical discourse.

With the existence of any given set of convictions, the range of interest is otherwise. The psychologist or sociologist is mainly interested in convictions as symptoms. To him, the conviction reported by a subject or characterizing a group is significant not so much for its own integrity as for the emotional and social experiences it betrays. The rhetorician, on the other hand, is interested in convictions not alone as symptoms, but as communications too. The force of the conviction, the manner of its expression, the impact that it has or promises to have—the whole metabolism of the disputed idea is within the province of the rhetorician. Thus it is that the elusive concept, *clusters of opinion*, must be accounted for in rhetorical terms. Admittedly, our level of generalization in the foregoing paragraphs has been quite abstract. The universe is not as neatly departmentalized as the academic polity, and distinctions among approaches to a subject cannot always be made without strain. Yet the distinctions are sometimes useful, and may serve in the present case to justify our approach to a subject that claims the attention of more than one scholarly discipline.

In attempting to clarify the clustering of opinions, we must return to the concept of argumentative synthesis, and we can do so by noting one characteristic of the three paradigms of argument that were examined earlier: length. The *Apologia* of Newman, the Lincoln-Douglas debates, and the Platonic dialogues are all works of substantial quantity, certainly longer than what we ordinarily regard as a speech. This length is both requisite to and revealing of the strategy of argumentative synthesis. The *Apologia*, for example, is almost certainly better able than a single speech or short essay to perform an argumentative synthesis because of its length. Because of its length, the *Apologia* can approach the condition of a novel in one important respect: it can create and populate a universe of its own, one that maintains internal consistency in obedience to its own rules of decorum. There are two aspects in which this work can be considered that, taken together, determine its plausibility, its rhetorical strength, its power to solicit uncommitted auditors to accept this universe as their own. These are the aspects of style and coherence. Style refers to the multitude of linguistic tactics that constitute the compositional detail of the work. Coherence refers to the internal consistency of the work, to the rightness or propriety with which it orders and justifies the experiences it itself evokes, and to its capacity for raising and then satisfying its auditors' expectations according to some hierarchy of values that it progressively discloses to them.

Newman, in the *Apologia*, was able to create a coherent universe. Once his auditors were induced to accept a few conditional premises of that universe, the rest of it followed. The universe needed only to be coherent with and argumentatively compatible with these conditional premises. Given some length of composition or some substantial amount of time with his auditors—which really, in the end, amount to the same thing—the rhetor can create a new universe of discourse and, in so doing, more thoroughly persuade his auditors in many details of his doctrine.

Lincoln's Second Inaugural address is an interesting specimen to consider with regard to argumentative synthesis because it is an exception to the rule of length. It is a brief speech by the standards of Lincoln's time, too brief, it would seem, to create a universe of discourse. Yet it discloses a cluster of opinions which was certainly alien to the auditors of 1865 in its detachment from chauvinism, its historical perspective, and its pervasive sense of tragedy. Add to the list the tone of compassion in the speech and its rejection of retributive justice, and a universe begins to take shape. It was a universe of discourse that few of Lincoln's auditors ever finally inhabited, but that does not deter us, a century later, from finding the speech highly meritorious. It is true that the policies of reconstruction that followed Lincoln's death can be regarded as evidence that his views failed to take hold, hence that he was a rhetorical failure. But we must equally bear in mind that he was twice elected to the presidency, and he is now an incomparable national hero. The rhetorical triumphs are more striking than the rhetorical failures. These triumphs, and especially the increasing enhancement of his reputation after his death, can be illuminated by reference to argumentative synthesis. Lincoln created a coherent universe in which major public issues were arranged in an hierarchy of order and thus were brought under linguistic control. His reputation has been enhanced as his universe of discourse is clarified through the exegesis of his speeches and writings. Such clarification does take time, and that may be one reason for our thinking better of Lincoln's speeches than did many of his contemporaries.[14] In any event, although the strategy of argumentative synthesis does require a certain quantitative latitude for its perfection, it can serve as a critical instrument for single speeches, as our earlier consideration of Chapman's Coatesville Address illustrated.

---

[14] See, Earl W. Wiley, "Buckeye Criticism of the Gettysburg Address," *Speech Monographs*, XXIII (March 1956), pp. 1–8.

After all, no man designs even a single, brief discourse in some insulated compartment of his mind. All the resources of the rhetor, however modest they may be, are brought to bear on the act of composition, however modest it may be. The result may be plodding or unimaginative or inhibited, but whatever its character it has involved the whole man; anything that he believes or disbelieves can have a bearing on it. The rhetor may confine his discourse to a niggling subject of small consequence, but that subject may be a part of a larger cluster of opinions in his own mind. The limits of time or space, the requirements of the moment, the repressions of a taciturn temperament, any one of a hundred factors can restrict the point of view a man chooses to incorporate into a discourse, but that does not mean that the point of view he presents is all he has, or that it has not been decisively shaped by the rest of what he believes. The single discourse probably cannot disclose a universe of discourse, but it will often be a symptom of such a universe existing in the rhetor's mind. Such a presumption, at least, may help the critic account for the single discourse.

We can now see that the argumentative synthesis and the cluster of opinions we found to be a recurrent characteristic of belief are really two sides of the same coin. Argumentative synthesis is a strategy of the rhetor in ordering and subsuming the issues of a controversy under a general point of view. The cluster of opinions is a synthesis viewed as belief and disbelief. The focus of one is on the discourse; the focus of the other is on the auditor. When we have found opinions arranged in a certain synoptic order in a discourse, we have called it argumentative synthesis. When we have found them arranged in the same order within the mind of a man, we have called it a cluster of opinions. Having seen the relationship between the two, we can now apply a principle disclosed by our former consideration of exhortation, and postulate that insofar as the argumentative synthesis being urged by a rhetor coincides with the cluster of opinions being held by his auditor, this rhetor's word will receive increasing credit from those auditors until he becomes for them a prophet—that is, his word alone will be sufficient argument for them. He will have the power to persuade those auditors in details of their common doctrine by his pronouncement alone. To have the status of prophet, the rhetor must be regarded by his auditors as, in some way, the source of the synthesis they have accepted. For the rhetor merely to pronounce the tenets of their common doctrine is not enough to make him a prophet; unless he is somehow regarded as responsible for that doctrine, he is only a mimetic-orator.

Joseph McCarthy will exemplify the prophetic effect. In his relatively long campaign of propaganda, he was able to create a universe. His universe had coherence. It explained and justified the anxieties it helped to engender. It imposed an order on the experiences of its auditors—experiences it helped supply—and related these experiences to an objective reality: the "Communist conspiracy." Because McCarthy was able to create a universe of discourse, his rhetorical power extended beyond carrying one argument or another in a routine controversy; he was able to win a faithful following, and to graduate into prophecy.

One final determination remains to be made concerning argumentative synthesis, and that is what makes one synthesis more attractive than another if both are equally coherent. Why do the discourses of Lincoln still have force and the power to move while those of Douglas are little more than historical monuments? The answers lie in the other aspect, besides coherence, of a synthetic universe of discourse: style. Style makes the difference between two equally coherent syntheses. We could display the difference between Lincoln and Douglas by enumerating the hundreds of superior details in the compositions of the former over the latter. This would be the procedure of the critic. And here we are able to derive a general formula from our consideration of argumentative discourse: it is coherence that will determine the range and intensity of effect of argumentative discourse; it is style that will determine the preferability of one set of argumentative discourses to its competitors. Or, to put it more succinctly: coherence determines absolute effects, style determines relative effects.

Obviously, the relative effects must precede the absolute effects; an auditor must accept the conditional premises of a universe of discourse in preference to competing premises before he will enter into the universe and begin inhabiting it. Douglas says popular sovereignty is the paramount concept, and all other current political problems can be subsumed under it. Lincoln says slavery is wrong; that is the main issue, and all other issues are subordinate to it. Assuming that Douglas and Lincoln had actually achieved the syntheses implied by these statements, the audience would have been confronted with a choice of conditional premises, either *if Popular Sovereignty, then all else that Douglas represents follows* or *if slavery is wrong, then all else that Lincoln represents follows*. The struggle of the two rhetors would have been to gain acceptance of their respective premises, and he whose stylistic tactics were effective would have gained the audience's assent. Other ideas, related to the premise as co-constituents in an argumentative synthesis, would have followed in its wake, and that particular rhetorical competition would have been effectively over. Indifference or intransigence rather than contrariness would then have been the rhetor's main impediment. He would no longer have had to struggle against disbelief; unbelief would have been his only barrier to the control of that audience; that and the danger of apostasy.

In graduating into the condition in which unbelief rather than disbelief is his main enemy, the rhetor more nearly approaches the condition of the poet with respect to his audience, and it is interesting to note that his discourse too will likely approach more closely the epideictic tone.

If there is any rhetorical competition after the relative effects have been determined, that is, after an auditor has accepted the premises of a universe, that competition is among those who share the premises. In sum, the competition is among the faithful. Competing points of view will claim the sanction of the same premises, and the argumentative procedures will become more clearly enthymematic. What must be noted is that in situations where the strategy of argumentative synthesis is at work, enthymemes do not begin to figure importantly in the controversy until after some set of premises has been established as convictions of the auditors, and established with relatively deep and abiding intensity. Once these premises have been established, there can follow the heresies, doctrinal disputes, purifications of faith, and mimetic-oratory that characterize an established universe of discourse.

SUMMARY

Our consideration of Newman, Plato, and the Lincoln-Douglas debates, of argumentative incompatibility, of the synthetic universe of discourse, and of clusters of opinion has constituted an attempt to examine a genre of rhetorical discourse: argumentation. This genre would be located somewhere near the center of our hypothetical scale of rhetorical discourses, and we have so defined the genre that it would include a large number of discourses, at least in the history of American public address. Fortunately for us, argumentative discourse is much more common in the United States than, for example, exhortation. It is, at least, as of this writing; rhetorical conditions can change. For the purposes of exploration, our conception of this genre has been gross; that is, we have not discriminated among the types of discourses within the genre. One could do so with further study. Indeed, the degree of refinement that we give to the points along our scale will be an arbitrary matter, for no two discourses are exactly alike—even the repetition of a speech will occur in a different situation; so one could, with unlimited time and vast quantities of information, assign a place on the scale to each individual rhetorical discourse, and thus see it in relation to every other rhetorical discourse. Obviously, this is only a theoretical possibility; such a degree of refinement is not only impractical, it is not even especially desirable. If, as we have assumed throughout this book, one of the major objectives of rhetorical criticism is to enrich our understanding of the rhetorical uses of language, critics can probably do their work better by seeing and disclosing the elements common to many discourses rather than the singularities of a few.

It is because our focus has been on the genre rather than the individual discourse that we have been led to consider the argumentative process. Rather than attempt to gauge the effects of the single discourse on its immediate audience, which would be the tendency of the neo-Aristotelian critic, we have instead sought to discern the effects of the whole process of argument, and we have in consequence seen these effects as sequential: different at different stages of the argumentative process. We have assumed the single discourse to be part of a historic process of argument, one that, in the cases of some subjects, has never really ended, but has instead passed into new phases. In viewing specimens of argument, our account has only arrested this process at given moments in its development.

The process has been our theme—the process by which, through the medium of language, a private attitude becomes a public faith. Patently, in attempting to illustrate how the rhetorical critic may proceed, we have raised more questions than we have answered. We have not evolved any system of rhetorical criticism, but only, at best, an orientation to it. An orientation, together with taste and intelligence, is all that the critic needs. If his criticism is fruitful, he may end with a system, but he should not, in our present state of knowledge, begin with one. We simply do not know enough yet about rhetorical discourse to place our faith in systems, and it is only through imaginative criticism that we are likely to learn more.